CHRISTIANITY AND THE LAW OF SEPARATION

Dr. Byron Hardy

ISBN 979-8-88751-194-8 (paperback)
ISBN 979-8-88751-195-5 (digital)

Copyright © 2023 by Dr. Byron Hardy

All rights reserved. No part of this publication may be reproduced, distributed, or transmitted in any form or by any means, including photocopying, recording, or other electronic or mechanical methods without the prior written permission of the publisher. For permission requests, solicit the publisher via the address below.

Christian Faith Publishing
832 Park Avenue
Meadville, PA 16335
www.christianfaithpublishing.com

Printed in the United States of America

CONTENTS

Introduction vii

Law of Separation 1
Biblically Based Counseling as a Component of
Separated Discipleship 11
Intentionally Direct Therapy (IDT) 19
New Creations 21
Thoughts about 3D Christianity 26
Secular Psychotherapy 28
The Authority of Scripture 37
Biblical Inerrancy 40
Sufficiency of Scripture 42
As Inerrancy Speaks to the Rule of Faith, so
Sufficiency Speaks to the Rule of Practice 44
General and Special Revelation, as It Reveals the
Majesty of God, within the Counseling Process 46
Five Influential Counseling Books to Consider 49
Disciples of Jesus Christ Should Not Make the
Claim "You Cannot Really Love God Unless You
Love Yourself" 55
The Sovereignty of God and Its Importance to
the Counseling Process 58
Sovereignty of God and Free Will of Man 61

Defining the Providence of God and Its
Importance in the Counseling Process............................63
Defining the Justice of God..65
Defining the Love of God 68
Counseling with Those Who Fear World Events 71
Importance of James 4:1–5 for Marital Counseling..........74
Are Trials an Indication that God Is Punishing Us?.........76
Common Psychotherapy Labels..79
Verbally Abusive Behavior (Husband to Wife) in
a Marriage 84
Dynamics of Forgiveness..86
Workaholic Personality...88
Hope for the Anxious...90
Transferring Our Faith to Our Children..........................93
Marital Intimacy 95
Regret Over Past Sin...97
Authority and Sufficiency of Scripture (Bibliology) 99
God the Father (Theology Proper) 101
What the Fatherhood of God Does in Our Lives...........103
Attributes of God 105
Decrees of God 108
God the Son (Christology) 110
Deity of Jesus 112
Humanity of Jesus Christ 114
God the Holy Spirit (Pneumatology)..............................116
The Trinity...118
The Ministry of the Holy Spirit in the Context of
Counseling...121
Describe the Ministry of the Holy Spirit in
Relation to the Will of God..123
Ministry of the Holy Spirit in Relation to God's Word...125
Man (Anthropology) 127
Man's Current Condition 129

Depravity of Man 131
Present-Day Self-Esteem Theology 133
Believer's New Identity in Christ 136
Salvation (Soteriology) 138
Why It Is Ethical to Talk about the Gospel in a
Counseling Session 140
Importance of Bringing a Counselee to Christ 142
The Role of Baptism 144
Greater Intimacy with God 146
Satan (Demonology) 148
Satan, the Great Deceiver 150
The Church (Ecclesiology) 152
Biblical Counseling Does Not Fall under the
Authority of Psychology 155
Active Church Participation Is Vital for the
Counselor and Counselee 157
Christian Living (Practical Theology) 159
How Does Biblical Counseling Relate to the
Biblical Mandate of Discipleship? 161
Sanctification Is a lifelong Process, Not a One-
Time Event 163
Marriage and Family (Biblical Sociology) 165

Appendix 175
Annotated Bibliography 181

INTRODUCTION

(For Christianity and the Law of Separation)

The book you are about to read is birthed from hours and hours of research on the topic of Biblically Based Counseling. Although Biblical Counseling was the catalyst for this study and eventual book, there is no doubt that the information here may be applied to all aspects of Christian Discipleship. Please don't let the term counseling or the idea of research for counseling keep you from reading the pages and discovering the fundamental nature of Christian discipleship.

You may also find the term Biblically based to be an interesting concept. By using this term, I am suggesting that everything we do, whether it is worship, counseling, or even recommending a resource to a person in need, be Biblically based. All things within our lives must be based on Christ Jesus. God's Word, the Bible, allows us to speak the truth about Jesus while we minister in the marketplace. All sixty-six books contained in the Bible point people toward Jesus. So there is a great need for every step we make on life's journey, to be Biblically based.

In a way, this narrative is a back-to-the-basics approach to Christianity. From the Law of Separation to the author's moving away from Christian Counseling and the desire for the Trinity to be known to the basics of scripture, all who read these words will see Jesus as the basic cornerstone of Christianity. Afterall, if it wasn't for Jesus's shed blood and His saving grace, we could not and would not be called Christ followers, Christians. All aspects and concepts in this book flow in a widespread plethora of love expressed from the one true God toward us as humans.

Jesus is all we will ever need. He is the supreme ruler and ultimate judge of the universe. The Christian trinity is the only true God by which man might be saved from the throes of hell. Several scriptures warn the Christian community about a great falling away which must take place before the return of Jesus Christ. Let us heed these warnings and ensure that the next generation has the opportunity to hear about Jesus. The content of this book will hopefully allow you to speak to this generation and help them find Jesus and their need of a Savior.

So sit back read and enjoy. Yes, you will critique and maybe even criticize some of my writings and thoughts, but please put that aside. The older I get, the more I realize that all I really desire from life is for everyone to be a fully devoted disciple of Jesus. Go back to your basics and rediscover the One who put in place, the Law of Separation.

Byron Hardy; D. Min.

LAW OF SEPARATION

As we wander deeper into the twenty-first century, it is evident that as Christians, we must conscientiously, physically, and spiritually separate ourselves from the ideations of the pagan world. Too often, we find ourselves, our children, and our grandchildren, with our cognition in the world, struggling with a commitment to the one true God. When we accept Jesus as Savior and Lord, we contractually agree to be light, within the darkness of humanity. For us to consider a detachment from the world and its dark spaces, we must consider the law of separation.

When we discuss the law of separation, we are not talking about a law of nonfellowship with the world. Although we must separate ourselves from the sinful nature of the world, we still must have fellowship with those who are on the outside (Colossians 4:5). There is, however, a demarcation between fellowship with the world and an acceptance of the practices and sin nature of the world.

For us to separate ourselves, spiritually and at times physically, from the paganized world, we must abide in Christ. Jesus is preeminent. He is above all gods. He is above all matters of life. He is the ruler of all things. It is because of Jesus coming to live among us and to take our place on the cross that we must consider the law of separation. Christians are called to be a different species, a different variety, from those creatures who live in the world. Jesus is known as one of a kind; He is the first person in a new race of humans. As creatures in this human race, we are to emulate Jesus.

All through the Bible, the word of God, you will witness the law of separation. We initially observe this law in Genesis 1. When we consider the six (6) days of creation, we see separation. Light versus darkness, heaven is separated from the earth, the land is separated from the sea, and the day is separated from the night. There is even a separation of the species of the air and the sea. Separation is present at the creation of the world.

When we consider mankind, the greatest of all of God's created beings, we think of the call of separation placed upon the life of Abraham. Abraham is called to distinguish himself from his local people in the Ur of the Chaldeans. Abraham was obedient to this act of separation even though there was a huge price to pay. The act of true separation from the sins and pleasures of the world reveals to all regenerated Christians that there is a cost to following Jesus. As Abraham is given as an example for us, we see the price he paid to follow the God who called him to freedom from the world.

The law of separation asks us to abandon all for the sake of Jesus Christ. In fact, Matthew 10:37 (NKJV) makes a bold claim: if we love father or mother more than Jesus, we are not worthy of Him. Abraham knew this exact level of commitment. Ah, the law of separation calls us to a life of self-denial and into the pursuit of Jesus's life.

As we consider Abraham's descendants, we observe that God placed within them the law of separation. An illustration of this is when God decreed the command for the men of the Israelites to not marry foreign wives. Israel was to be a separated nation from all other nations, set apart and consecrated to God. When Israelite men married foreign women, against the authority of Almighty God, the law of separation was voided. When the law of separation is made null and void, all manners of sin creep into the camp.

Joshua 24 describes this for us. As you may know, this portion of scripture deals with a post-exodus, postconquest period within the nation of Israel. At the beginning of the chapter, Joshua calls the nation of Israel together. He does not call any other nations to be involved in the discussion. In Joshua's mind, by the hand of God, Joshua was only to deal with the people-group which was set aside to inhabit the promised land. God's call on Israel and now His call on us is dealing exclusively with the law of separation. "Thou shall have no other gods before me" (Exodus 20:3 KJV). Creator God desires only those in His fold who will be distinct from the paganized world.

As chapter 24 unfolds, Joshua reminds the people about their escape from Egypt. All through the forty-year journey to the promised land, God ensured that a remnant of the people would be solely dedicated to Him. Even as Israel fled Egypt, the Red Sea separated the chosen people of God from the demonized, Egyptian armies. Symbolism and physical reality prove to us that God wants a separated people unto Himself. As we study the journey out of Egypt, we apply to our lives the law of separation.

Joshua instructs the people to abandon the gods and idols of their forefathers and pursue only the one true God. They are to worship the God who created them. Joshua 24:15 requires Israel to make a choice—either they worship the gods who were on the back side of the Euphrates River, or they worship the God who delivered them out of Egypt. "But as for me and my house, we will serve the Lord." We must make the same choice; we either worship God or stay in a paganized state.

As we consider our Christian context and the forty-five thousand Christian denominations in the physical world, we do witness a Christian degree of separation. However, the extent of separation to which we are referring is not the separation from one denomination to another. No indeed. We are talking about the mandatory separation of regenerated Christians from a sin-infested world. While we may separate ourselves from other denominations due to styles of worship and doctrinal differences, the law of separation is clearly applied to us in the framework of being devoted to God and divorced from the world.

Let us consider Ephesians 5. Clearly, this chapter calls us to be light and to be separated from the darkness of the world. "You were once darkness but now you are light in the Lord." Our call to separation from the darkness of the world is as clear as day and night; it is as clear as the creation story in Genesis. Paul instructs the church at Ephesus to walk as children of light. As we read Paul's letter, we are challenged to be distinct from the world; we are challenged to separate ourselves psychologically, spiritually, and sometimes physically from the paganized world. We are not to have any fellowship with the unfruitful works of darkness.

Read Ephesians 5:11; it is forceful. We are not to fellowship with the world but are to expose the sinful nature and sinful acts of the world. Verse 12 moves even further, "For it is shameful even to speak of those things which are done by them in secret" (Ephesians 5:12 NKJV). Separation: we are now light; we must move away from the darkness. In fact, we are not even allowed to even hang out in the shadows. John 3:20 reminds us that men love darkness rather than light because their deeds are evil. If you are not separated from the darkness, your deeds are evil.

If we are called to be separate from the world, what do we gain by having a foot in the world? Why do we constantly love the world and the things in the world? First John 2:15 emphatically and forcefully says to not love the world of the things in the world. If anyone loves the world, the love of the Father is not in him. We want to desperately fit in with the world. Acceptance by people and the lack of courage on our part keep us attached to the desires of the world. However, as we study the law of separation, we know that we are called to be different from *all* aspects of the world ruled by Satan. Second Corinthians 4:4 says that the god of this age has blinded the eyes of those who are perishing. Separate yourself unto God, and you will not perish.

The book of Colossians speaks further to the life we are to live in Jesus. Jesus being preeminent, above all things, shed His blood on the cross so that we may live a life of separation. As mentioned earlier, once we accept Jesus's blood-giving act of separation, we enter into an agreement with God the Father. We do not have a choice. We must live a separate life—separation from sin, separation from the flesh, separation from the world, and separation from the pursuit of things that we need not and should not be doing.

How does this appear within the Christian lifestyle? Colossians chapter 3 opens with specific instructions for us. If we truly are of Christ's, then we are to not possess anger, not hold onto wrath, not have hatred toward each other, and ensure that filthy language is not gushing out of our mouths.

Yes, this is the law of separation. Christians are called to be different from the world.

During the '50s, '60s, and '70s, as Christians, we dressed and acted differently from the world. We demanded, at least in appearance, the necessity to be separated and detached from the things of the world. It was rare to go to movies, it was rare to drink alcohol, and it was very rare for a Christian to swear. While there may have been some legalism intertwined into the Christian life during this time period, there was still an understanding that Christians were to be different from the world in appearance, practice, and lifestyle. The call to separation may be a forgotten law within Christianity.

Philippians 2 says that Jesus humbled Himself and became obedient to death even the death of the cross. Why? Because Jesus set into place the law of separation. Jesus's shed blood on the cross is the borderline between Christians and pagans. His shed blood is the borderline between light and darkness. His shed blood establishes the borderline between heaven and hell. Jesus also meant for us to live the victorious Christian life in the here and now. Jesus calls us to be separated from the evil of the world and to be separated unto His life. As we gain spiritual separation, we gain victory over the paganized world.

Ephesians 6:10–18 gives us the offensive weapons required of us to live unto Christ, to live a victorious Christian life, and to be separated from the world. These weapons are not available to the dark entities of the world. Furthermore, 2 Corinthians 10:4–5 argues for us to retain the power from our spiritual weapons and to use this power to pull down strongholds that interfere with our capacity to be separated from the world.

CHRISTIANITY AND THE LAW OF SEPARATION

In the twenty-first century, we see the effects of not adhering to the law of separation. As parents and grandparents to the next generation, we have not performed well at being the gatekeepers for our families and our Christian worldview. Many things have crept into the faith. Several Christians are now living in a premarriage state with non-Christians. There are those who believe that Jesus's shed blood will save "all within the human race [universalism]." There is a belief that a one-sentence *sinner's* prayer accompanied by a dunk in the baptismal tank will save someone from eternity in hell. As gatekeepers, if we are not separated from the world, if we are not teaching the truth of Jesus, many who follow us will undeniably not be gatekeepers. In essence, the gate is wide open, and no one will monitor the gate. Shut the gate now and do not allow any more evil to creep into our Christian families.

It is spiritually impossible to be in two camps. You cannot be of God and attempt to live in the world. The camp of the world is Satan's camp. Why would you attempt to stay in that world? There is darkness, and there is light; that's it. We either live in the light, or we live in the darkness. There is not any in-between. Jesus came to give us freedom, to give us light, and to restore us to the creator. He reconciles us to the Father. Our call is to be separated unto God.

Colossians 2:11 argues further about engagement with the law of separation. Circumcision made without hands is the context of this portion of the Bible. The Israelite men were called to physical circumcision—the mark of separation as it were from all the other pagan nations. Israelite males were commanded to be circumcised or face banishment from the nation of Israel. Either way, these men were separated to God or separated from God.

As Christians, physical circumcision is no longer valid. However, the circumcision of the heart is valid. We are crucified with Christ (Galatians 2:20). When we engage in this crucifixion, our spiritual hearts are marked; they are circumcised. We now have a marking in the spiritual realm. This marking separates us from the world of Satan. Paul calls us to put off the sins of the world and put on the righteousness of Christ. The circumcision which cannot be physically seen, the circumcision of the heart, is what separates us from the world. In 2 Corinthians 5:17, "Therefore if any man be of Christ, he is a new creation, old things have passed away… all things have now become new."

Christians are called to be different from the world. We are called to separate ourselves from the world. It matters how we act, it matters what comes out of our mouths, and it matters where we go, what we do, and how we interact with one another. We are called to love one another. First John 4:7–8 calls us to brotherly love because love is of God. If we do not love one another, the love of the Father is not in us, and we are not considered to be one of His separated creatures. Love within Christianity is first, and then we move out into the world. Christian love separates us from the unloving world.

So, as Christ was crucified on the cross, to be the substitutionary sacrifice for us, we are too to be crucified with Him. We are crucified to self-nature, we are crucified to sin, and we are crucified to the pagan world. Galatians 2:20 states, "I am crucified with Christ; it is no longer 'I' but Christ who lives in me." The law of separation is understood here. Romans 6 instructs us to not sin just so that grace may abound. Sin is at the least to be abated in our lives and hopefully shut out altogether. Repentance means to turn our backs on the pleasures of the world and stay completely focused on the life of Jesus Christ.

The life of Jesus Christ allows us to move away from sin, be separated from the world, and live the victorious Christian life. If we are separated, why do we continue to sin? Paul asks this at the beginning of Romans 6. If we are buried with Christ, into the newness of life, we are separated from the lure of the world. When we are physically baptized with water, we are saying to the witnesses present and to the world at large that we are now separated from the world. It is a marking of separation. It is the law of separation in action. We are, according to Romans 6, crucified with Christ, that the body of sin might be dealt away with; therefore, we are no longer slaves of sin. Jesus's act of separation on the cross gives us freedom.

Colossians 2:13–15 shows us that we are made alive together with Jesus. When we are regenerated, we have a new birth, there is a new covenant that is placed onto our hearts. John 3:5 speaks to Christians being born of the spirit which causes us to be renewed. We no longer have a heart toward the things of Satan, the sin which has weighed us down; we now have a heart toward those things of God.

These discussion points, on the law of separation, are crucial as we draw nearer to the return of Jesus Christ. We must understand separation from the world if we wish to persevere to the end. Many portions of scripture warn us about the great falling away, which will occur prior to the return of Jesus. Regardless of one's hermeneutic on this subject, we must agree on the fact that this falling away will wreak havoc within the Christian community.

Out of the many cited scriptures, referring to the great falling away, Luke 8 (sower and the seed), 1 Timothy 4,

Matthew 24, 2 Thessalonians 2, Colossians 1, Jude, 2 Peter, and Hebrews 6, we will focus on 2 Timothy 3:1–9. Please take the time to read this section of the Bible.

Second Timothy 3 opens with a staggering exposé on the human condition. As we review the opening verse, we see the words "in the last days." How do we define this term? It is defined as we go further into the text. By definition, the transpiring of events, as written, defines the term "in the last days." As we read, we may infer that we are in the last days due to the mental checkboxes being "marked-off" within the text. Are men lovers of themselves? CHECK. Are they lovers of money? CHECK. Boasters, proud, blasphemers, disobedient? CHECK, CHECK, CHECK, CHECK. You get the picture. Your hand gets tired from checking off the boxes.

And yet, verses 10–17 of 2 Timothy 3 entice us back to the law of separation. Paul endorses the disciplines noted in the life of Timothy, the disciplines of separation. Timothy has separated himself from the things of the world, specifically, from the sin that so easily besets us. Verse 14 is very poignant as Paul implores Timothy (and now us), to "continue in the things which you have learned and been assured of."

The distinction, then for us, is to be separated from the world and separated in the direction of the one true God, His Son Jesus, and the indwelling Holy Spirit.

BIBLICALLY BASED COUNSELING AS A COMPONENT OF SEPARATED DISCIPLESHIP

Being a disciple of Jesus Christ is a lifelong activity. We have the mandate in Matthew 28 and Mark 16 to make disciples of Jesus Christ. In Matthew 4:19, Jesus says to His core group of disciples that He will make them fishers of men. There was a clear understanding that the role of Jesus's inner circle of disciples was to replicate themselves into others who then would become new followers of Jesus Christ. Discipleship existed in the early teachings of Jesus and the early church. Since the inception of the church of Jesus Christ, discipleship has always been the focus and will of God. Discipleship is following and practicing the teachings in God's word.

If you think about it, conversion—that is, accepting Jesus Christ as Lord and Savior—is only step one within a lifetime of being Jesus's disciple. Whether you call this initial step of becoming a disciple "getting saved" or being regenerated, it must occur prior to anyone being a true disciple of Jesus Christ. We are not talking about saying the sinner's prayer; we mean that for you to become Jesus's disciple, you must have your inner man or woman changed. Regeneration, the moment you become a disciple, is defined as the admittance of perpetual sin within humanity, specifically the individual human, and the need for humanity to accept Jesus's death on the cross as the solution to perpetual sin. This acceptance of the ultimate solution is the action required to convert a sinner into a saint.

We see a beautiful picture of discipleship in Luke 9:23. *"Then he [Jesus] said to them all, "If anyone wants to become my follower, he must deny himself, take up his cross daily, and follow me."*[1] If we truly wish to follow Jesus and be His disciple, we pick up our cross and follow Him. This is where biblically based counseling comes into the picture. When people struggle with the concept of following Jesus, when people struggle with sin and taking up their cross, we sit with them and reveal to them the biblical pattern of discipleship. In order to follow Jesus, to be His true disciple, we deny ourselves and give Jesus the permission to lead our lives. Jesus must be Lord.

Disciples of Jesus need to be taught these concepts. Biblically based counseling is an opportunity for these teachings to take place. We accept the rejection of the world each day and follow the one true God. Biblically based counseling speaks this truth into the life of the disciple of Jesus.

John 14:26 gives hope that needs to be passed on through the counseling process. The Holy Spirit teaches all things (everything) to all people. As Holy Spirit teaches, there are times when, as counselors, we come alongside fellow disciples to help them navigate these teachings. We exhort, admonish, and give correction where necessary. God the

---

[1] Unless otherwise noted, all scriptures are taken from the New English Translation Bible, Full Notes Edition (Thomas Nelson, 1996).

CHRISTIANITY AND THE LAW OF SEPARATION

Father gives complete provision for every disciple of Jesus, for every situation of life. Counselors know this, understand this, and point counselees toward biblical answers. All of this forms a piece of discipleship.

Biblical counseling is rooted in the word of God. Thoroughly grounding itself in discipleship, biblical counseling points wayward disciples back to the cross of Christ. Second Timothy 3:16–17 reminds us that all scripture is profitable for doctrine, teaching, and correcting the disciple of Jesus Christ. Colossians 1:28–29 is a call to teach every person, warn every person, and present them to Jesus who is the perfecter of the individual's faith. These verses prove how biblical counseling fits succinctly into the mandate of discipleship.

We are all born into a sinful condition. We are not born into a state of being a disciple of Jesus Christ. From the moment we are born, until the moment we accept Jesus Christ as Lord and Savior, we are considered to be sinners. Due to the fall of the human race as recorded in Genesis chapter 3, the sin nature clearly exists in all people. Just look around you at the lawlessness which exists in the twenty-first century.

At this point in history, men and women are doing what comes naturally to them. The natural accomplishment for man and woman is to sin. Sure, we can marginalize the sin nature and attempt to convince ourselves that past definitions of sin are antiquated and inaccurate, but in reality, it is the sin nature that keeps us from being reconciled to a Holy God. The sin nature, by definition, means we are not naturally disciples of Jesus Christ.

Individuals' natural tendency is to be separated from their creator and to desire separation from the said creator.

Adam and Eve were created in the image of God and yet chose to rebel against the creator (Genesis 3:1–7). Due to the corruption which ensued from the "fall of man," in their unholy, natural state, no one can appease a Holy God. Natural (sinful) man does not understand the things of God (1 Corinthians 2:14). There is no healthy spiritual sensitivity within the heart of a person who has not been regenerated or restored to a right relationship with their creator. Therefore, one's spirit is completely separated from God the creator. Prior to becoming a disciple of Jesus, all people live in spiritual darkness. Matthew 6:23 tells us that the darkness in man is great; it is contrary to the hope offered to us through Jesus Christ.

Separation is a horrible thing. When friends and family members die, we grieve due to the separation. There is a parallel here to our lives with God. Due to being separated from the Holy God, death from sin brings grief into our lives. Separation from God causes spiritual death and inner sorrow. It is only through the shed blood of Jesus that regeneration and reconciliation will occur (John 3:16–21). Everlasting life is available to fallen humanity. Humans are no longer separated from the creator when there is spiritual restoration.

When we describe "human nature," we are describing the inner core of people. In a worldly setting, fundamental beliefs of feelings, psychology, and the way people think form a piece of this description. Human nature in itself is sinful. Sin within the human race dictates that there is absolutely nothing anyone can do, via their own merit, to connect with a Holy God.

It is important to state here, and flesh out later, that secular psychotherapy does not belong within the context of biblical counseling. Psychotherapy is rooted in human philosophy. If people are by nature evil and sinful, how can anything derived from the minds of man be healthy for the counseling process? Psalm 14:1–3 and Romans 3:10–12 tell us that all people reject God, and as a result, all are morally corrupt.[2]

We (humans) are so ungodly. Jesus came to earth to be the propitiation between a Holy God and an unholy man (1 John 4:10). There had to be this link in the relationship. Men love darkness rather than light because their deeds are evil and morally corrupt (John 3:19). By default, the existing condition of every person's nature is to embrace evil intent. Jesus as the light of the world shines in the darkness and exposes the sin nature of each human being (John 8:12). True disciples of Jesus Christ understand this concept. Without regeneration and the act of propitiation, one cannot be a disciple of Jesus.

Man is separated from God. If man's nature is depicted as being sinful, then his condition is depicted as being lost in his sinful state. The spiritual condition of man is further defined as being corrupt. Corruption cannot inherit the kingdom of God. When we speak of being lost, we recognize spiritual death is present. Sin has caused men to be separated from a Holy God. This separation means that we are living on the cusp of eternal death. Romans 5:12 speaks specifically about death being present in unregenerate man.

We know from Romans 6:23 that the wages of sin, or the sinful condition, is death. Ephesians 2:1 gives us hope that while we were dead to sins, we now are able to be alive in Christ. As mentioned above, Romans 5:12 says that death

---

[2] *New English Translation Bible*, Full Notes Edition (Thomas Nelson, 1996).

has come to all people due to the sinful condition of their hearts.

With sin being the enemy of our soul, we comprehend that the only solution to escaping eternal death is through the shed blood of Jesus. Hebrews 9:22 makes the claim that without the shedding of blood, there is not any remission of sins. First John 1:8 reminds us that if we believe we do not have a sinful nature, we are being deceived. There must be a recognition of this condition. It is through this recognition that regeneration may take place.

Due to the sinful, lost condition of man, there is, according to Galatians 5:17, a war being waged between flesh and spirit. The apostle Paul further claimed in Romans 7:18 that there was nothing good in him. Paul recognized the need for regeneration to occur in his life and therefore reconciled to his creator. Paul did not wish for separation to continue between God and himself. Genesis 3 is the record of the fall of man. Romans 7 is a testament to the fallen, sinful, corrupt condition, causing us to fight this spiritual battle.

Due to the fall of man, as noted in Genesis 3, all people are born with a sin nature. Without the assistance of the indwelling Holy Spirit, it is impossible for anyone created by the Holy God to avoid being engaged in sin. The depravity of man indicates that man is fallen and corrupt in nature. This is due to the original sin occurring within the garden of Eden.

On our own, it is impossible for us to avoid sin and follow the commandments of a Holy God. Jeremiah 17:9 tells us that the heart of man is deceitful above all things and desperately wicked. Ephesians 2:1–3 says that we are dead in our trespasses and sins. By nature, and due to the fall, we are children of wrath. Depravity means to be wicked and morally corrupt. It is important for the biblically based counselor to present this belief to the person being counseled (counselee). Without Jesus's shed blood and the indwelling Holy Spirit, no one can alter their depraved, corrupt state. The indwelling of the Holy Spirit must be present in all people for the depravity of their souls to be purified.

When we make disciples of Jesus Christ, we must present the definition of depravity to the individual being taught. Depravity in the human race is wickedness personified. As previously noted, John 3:19 expressly states that men love darkness rather than light because their deeds are evil. Corruption and depravity are the natural inclinations and defaults that people will gravitate toward as they navigate their lives. First Corinthians 2:14 tells us that the natural (depraved) man does not understand the things of the Holy God.

We pray and hope that the response to the presentation of Jesus as Savior and reconciler for humans to the creator God is the acknowledgment by the counselee that they are sinful, corrupt persons. Secular psychotherapy does not bring this corrupt state into the conversation. Inherently, psychotherapy believes people are good and righteous. It is only through personal confession of Jesus as Lord and Savior that man's inherent, sinful nature may be restored. Biblically based counseling and not psychotherapy must present this truth. In *Acts 4:12*, *"And there is salvation in no one else. For there is no other name under heaven given among people by which we must be saved."*[3]

---

[3] *New English Translation Bible*, Full Notes Edition (Thomas Nelson, 1996).

Due to the sinful, depraved nature of man, there is this chasm between God and His creation. We have need of a savior. Ephesians 2:8–9 explains to all that it is only the finished work of Jesus on the cross where wickedness in man may be eliminated. Yes, we continue to war after the flesh. However, we do have sanctification placed within us by the shed blood of Jesus. We are obligated to present to the counselee that if they genuinely wish to be free from their depraved/corrupt state, they must accept Jesus Christ as Lord and Savior. In John 8:36, if the Son has freed you, you are indeed free from your depraved life.

The condition of lost man may be further defined as alienation or separation from the God who created us. Philippians 2:15 gives evidence to the understanding that mankind, this generation, is corrupt. Ephesians 4:22–23 speaks to the old, sinful, lost man growing corrupt through deceitful lusts. Romans 6:11 makes the claim that we were dead to sin. Corruption exists as the condition of man.

INTENTIONALLY DIRECT THERAPY (IDT)

As we consider counseling and the word *therapy*, our thoughts might move us to some Freudian notion of psychological treatment. *Merriam-Webster* defines therapy as "therapeutic medical (medicinal) treatment of impairment, injury, disease or disorder. Furthermore, the psychotherapist knows all actions in therapy are messages that need to be decoded and understood regardless of the language the patient uses."[4] From a biblical counseling perspective, therapy may be defined as the application of Holy Spirit—inspired teaching which hopefully emerges as healing within the life of the counselee. When the one to whom therapy is provided submits their life, including the repentance from sin, to God Almighty, spiritual healing will supernaturally take place.

We may also consider the term therapy within the context of Christianity as our Christian worldview. Intentionally direct therapy suggests that the "black-and-white" commands of the Bible and our need to obey these commands must be

---

[4] Retrieved from https://merriam-webster.com/dictionary/therapy (July 2021).

presented within the counseling process. Discipleship, after all, is the necessity to be a follower of Christ. When disciples obey and follow the commands of Jesus, which are given to us in His word, they will witness spiritual and inner healing in their lives. There is not a need for secular psychotherapy to be utilized in the life of the church and the disciples of Jesus.

IDT may be regarded by some as confrontational and even unloving. Blunt conversations within the Christian community are often viewed in this unloving context. However, as we consider the world and how it is moving toward a catastrophic demise, there must be this sense of urgency and bluntness in our lives as disciples of Jesus Christ.

Psalm 119:11 states, "Thy word have I hid in my heart that I might not sin against thee."

Within this biblical text is the appearance of urgency; I might not sin, speaks to this existing and present moment in time. In other words, if I have God's word(s) within me, it should keep me from immediate, current, and very present sin. Therefore, it stands to reason that although we are to be loving in all aspects of biblical counseling, there is also a necessity to be direct and potentially blunt when it comes to existing and perpetual sin in the life of the counselee.

NEW CREATIONS

Second Corinthians 5:17 is one of the prooftexts for being new creations in Jesus Christ. When we accept Jesus as savior, our old, spiritual lives die, and our spiritual lives then become regenerated. We recognize that all things are from God. When we accept God's plan of salvation, God the Father reconciles us to Him through the shed blood of Jesus Christ. Our identity is no longer viewed in terms of being corrupt but is viewed through the act of justification. Galatians 2:16 says we are vindicated or justified by Jesus Christ. Due to the shed blood of Jesus, the penalty for our sinful nature is removed (act of justification) from us.

Romans 6:4–11 speaks to our justified position in Christ. Once we accept Jesus, we walk in the newness of life. This is not the rebirth of physical life but of spiritual life. We are no longer slaves to sin but free from sin. The end of verse 11 tells us that we are alive in Christ. Ephesians 1:13–14 shows how the Holy Spirit brings newness into the repentant believer and then seals them for redemption.

Galatians 2:20 speaks of Christ physically being crucified. The apostle Paul moves this into a spiritual sense. Spiritually, Christ's crucifixion is regarded as though we were actually crucified with Christ. Once we accept Jesus, we have this new identity. We are moved from the category of a sinner and into the category of a saint. We now live, not in our own strength, but Christ's life in us brings about this newness. Jesus's supreme sacrifice is our only escape from the law, sin, and the power they have over our spiritual lives.

First Corinthians 15:46–58 gives a further glimpse into the realization that we have a new identity in Jesus. Through Adam (Romans 5:18–21), sin entered the world, and through sin came death. Jesus as the second Adam came to reverse this corruption. When we are considered heavenly beings (regenerated), we are changed. While our physical bodies are corrupted due to sin, our new identity in Christ allows our spiritual beings to be incorruptible. When we put on this incorruption (1 Corinthians 15: 54–55), we are new creations within the atoning work of Jesus on the cross.

Galatians 5:16 further speaks to our position in Christ. If we walk in the spirit, due to being regenerated, we will not fulfill the lusts of the flesh. When we do not fulfill the lusts of the flesh, the fruit of the spirit (Galatians 5:22–23) exists within our new selves. Verse 24 of Galatians 5 says that we who are Christ's put on the new identity of being crucified to the flesh.

Lordship

Adonai is the Hebrew word for Lord. Lord in a biblical context is interchangeable with the name Yahweh. In the Greek Septuagint translation of the Old Testament and the Greek translation of the New Testament, Kyrios is translated as Lord. In the New Testament, as an example, Thomas refers to Jesus as "My Lord and My God" (John 20:28).

CHRISTIANITY AND THE LAW OF SEPARATION

When we speak to the lordship of Jesus Christ, we are not referring to the name of the one true God. We are speaking directly to the requirement for Jesus to be the master over our lives. Yes, Jesus is Lord as in He is God, but He also must be the ruler and director of our lives. Philippians 2:9–11 shows us that one day, every knee will bow and demonstrate the quality of Lordship reigning in the ministry and life of Jesus Christ. We read, "As a result God highly exalted him and gave him the name that is above every name, so that at the name of Jesus every knee will bow—in heaven and on earth and under the earth—and every tongue confess that Jesus Christ is Lord to the glory of God the Father."[5]

As volunteer slaves of Jesus Christ, we yield our lives and our will to Him as the one true Lord. James, the half brother of Jesus, knew that he was a bondservant (slave) of Jesus Christ (James 1:1). When we concede to this slave position in Jesus, we are admitting the need for Jesus to be Lord. If we are the slaves, Jesus is the master. When we consider our lives, we know we are slaves to something. Either we are slaves to Jesus or we are slaves to sin (Romans 6:15–23).

Lordship is of prime importance in biblically based counseling. When we have the courage to accept Jesus Christ as Savior, we *must* have the courage to accept Him as the master and supervisor of our lives. When Jesus becomes our all in all, we can experience the victorious Christian life which He promised to us in John 10:10. We yield our free wills and thought processes to Jesus. Matthew 6:10, "Thy Will be done." In Acts 21:14, "The will of the Lord be done." There is submission to Jesus when we submit to His Lordship.

---

[5] *New English Translation Bible*, Full Notes Edition (Thomas Nelson, 1996).

Galatians 5:16 instructs us to walk in the spirit and, therefore, to not fulfill the lusts of the flesh. It is this lustful behavior that causes all of us to sin. We must emphasize to those seeking Jesus, both from a position of disciple and from a position of being lost, that there is a need for Jesus to direct and put order into their lives. When Jesus is master, we follow His teachings and the teachings of the Holy Spirit. Second Corinthians 10:5 instructs us to take every thought captive for us to be obedient to the lordship of Jesus. As Jesus is Lord and we are led by the Holy Spirit, will we be able to have our minds controlled by Him?

We see in Romans 7, where Paul understood the need for Jesus to be Lord of His life. Paul claimed that the things he should be doing and chasing, he was not accomplishing. The things in Paul's life, which he should not pursue, were in fact being achieved by him. In verse 25 of Romans 7, Paul recognizes the need for Jesus to be Lord. When Jesus is Lord of our lives, we move away from sin.

When we move away from sin, we become more sanctified. Sanctification is the act of being more Christlike as we seek His holiness. Lordship means that Jesus directs us. Lordship means that Jesus corrects us. Lordship means that Jesus gives us the courage to live the victorious Christian life.

Lordship teaches us that the Holy Spirit wants to bring us to Jesus. Through the advent of the Holy Spirit at Pentecost, Jesus now never leaves us. The hypostatic union, Jesus being both God and man, is of extreme importance to the world at large and specifically to the Christian in a Lord/disciple relationship. Jesus as the Son of God was the source of life and freedom as He walked on earth. We do not go to heaven to meet Jesus; He came to earth to meet us and to be our Lord. Jesus, due to His death on the cross, today comes to us as Lord.

As I was considering Lordship, the phrase "His only begotten son" came to mind. What does it mean for God to have given up His only begotten Son? How does this act of grace transpose itself into lordship? Does Jesus command lordship because of His sacrifice on the cross? Should only begotten actually be translated into one of a kind, which means it is this one-of-a-kind person who actually was given up to become our Lord and Savior?

Interestingly enough, as I was considering this thought, I came across a quote from Michael S. Heiser. Heiser claims, "It (only begotten) implies that there was a time when the Son did not exist—that he had a beginning… The term (Monogenes, translated in error as only begotten) literally means one-of-a-kind or unique. Consequently, Jesus…is unique among the Elohim who serve God."[6] It is through this assertion of Heiser's where we can claim that Jesus is indeed Lord. The "one-of-a-kind" God came to die for us and therefore deserves the attributes of Lord and also the command for us to follow Him as Lord.

---

[6] Michael S. Heiser, PhD, *The Unseen Realm: Recovering the Supernatural Worldview of the Bible* (Lexham Press, 2015).

THOUGHTS ABOUT 3D CHRISTIANITY

As the church is propelled into the darkness of the twenty-first century, it is apparent that true believers must hit a new dimension in their Christian experience. When we say a new dimension, we are not speaking to the bizarre notion that a new revelation is coming to the church. We are in fact speaking to the need for the Christian community to be ready for a potential end-of-time falling away.

There is about to be a great apostasy unleashed upon mankind that will influence the church. In Matthew 24:24 (ESV); "For false Christs and false prophets will arise and perform great signs and wonders, so as to lead astray, if possible, even the elect." How would a third dimension allow for readiness to exist within the body of Christ?

Two-dimensional Christianity is noticeable within the church. When we talk about two-dimensional Christianity, we are referring to the disciplines of reading/studying God's word while also petitioning the Lord in prayer. While studying God's word and meditating on the Bible through prayer are vital, there is however a third dimension that needs to be experienced by every believer.

The third dimension is the working and movement of the Holy Spirit within the Spirit-person of each believer.

CHRISTIANITY AND THE LAW OF SEPARATION

Ephesians 3:18 (NLT) claims: "And may you have the power to understand, as all God's people should, how wide, how long, how high, and how deep his love is." The power to understand things of God at this level may only be realized through the teaching of the Holy Spirit. In John 14:26, Jesus promised that the Holy Spirit will teach us all things.

How does this power manifest itself within the hearts of true children of God? (1 John 3:1, "Behold what manner of love the Father has bestowed upon us, that we should be called children of God! Therefore, the world does not know us because it did not know Him.") Acts 1:8 tells us that we shall receive power when the Holy Spirit comes upon us. The power we receive from the "upon" experience of the Holy Spirit allows us to be witnesses of the gospel of Jesus Christ in this dark and perverse generation.

Romans 14:17–18 (Expanded Bible) further instructs us,

> In the Kingdom of God, eating and drinking are not important [For the kingdom of God is not (about) eating and drinking]. The important things are living right with God [righteousness], peace and joy in the Holy Spirit. Anyone who serves Christ by living this way is pleasing God and will be accepted [approved; respected] by other people.

There is not any doubt that the third dimension of spirituality is essential to allow true Christians to endure to the end.

SECULAR PSYCHOTHERAPY

The Consideration to Remove This from "Christian Counseling"

At the core of what it is, psychotherapy in any form is not of God. Psychotherapy is the man-invented remedy for psychological anguish within the human mind. Original theories regarding the treatment of the distressed mind through psychotherapy and psychoanalysis may be credited to Josef Breuer and Sigmund Freud. When we consider their coauthored treatise, *Studies on Hysteria*[7], we quickly realize that this work is void of God. *Studies on Hysteria* may well suggest that Breuer and Freud were atheists.[8] By definition, atheists deny the existence of God.

Breuer and Freud give credence to the humanistic implementation of psychoanalysis and psychotherapy as possessing the capability to heal the traumatized soul and accompanying mind. If this is true, then God is not required

---

[7] J. Breuer and S. Freud, *Studies on Hysteria* (1895), Standard Edition, 2 (London: Hogarth Press, 1955).
[8] Ibid.

as a prerequisite for counseling or psychotherapy. However, if God is not considered within the hypotheses of secular psychotherapy, then we must state that pure, God-centered, Christian counseling should not embrace any form of secular psychotherapy. If Christian counseling continues to embrace theories derived from atheistic minds, we will not be able to witness genuine spiritual healing. As a biblically based counselor, this author desires to witness God-centered, spiritual healing within the world. Principles of man, such as psychotherapy, do not make allowance for God.

In his book *Shadowland*, author Thomas Horn states this about the atheistic teachings of Freudian theories and secular psychology.

> Freudianism might therefore be called the grandchild of the cult of Dionysus. Conversely, the person who gave himself over to the will of Dionysus was rewarded with unlimited psychological and physical delights… Human participants (in cultic Dionysus rituals) were sometimes subjected to the same orgiastic cruelty, as the rule of the cult was anything goes.[9]

If this is truly the case, we must at all costs flee from secular psychology and psychotherapy.

---

[9] Thomas R. Horn, *Shadowland: From Jeffrey Epstein to the Clintons, from Obama and Biden to the Occult Elite: Exposing the Deep-State Actors at War with Christianity, Donald Trump, and America's Destiny* (2019).

Breuer's hypothesis on the hypnoid state and theory of the need for psychoanalysis has links to modern-day terms and practices such as mindfulness, focusing, neurofeedback, and eye movement desensitization and reprocessing (EMDR).[10] These practices are not only taught in several seminaries, through the discipline of Christian counseling, but also employed, in clinical settings, by certified Christian counselors. In fact, this author's former Christian counseling association supports the ongoing use and training of these psychotherapy-directed disciplines.

Due to the essence and secularized nature of psychotherapy, it must be implicitly stated that psychotherapy does not belong in Christian seminaries and local churches, nor should it be inflicted upon God's children through counseling. Although there are several reasons for this author to exit the field of Christian counseling and psychotherapy, the ungodly teachings of secularism in Christian institutions are at the top of the list.

As an example, mindfulness, which is a substitution for meditating on the word of God, is void of the movement of the Holy Spirit. The writer of this paper has attended seminarian classes where this ritual was forced upon students each day. Mindfulness is psychotherapy in action. For edification purposes, a definition of mindfulness is warranted.

According to the *Greater Good Magazine*, published by the Greater Good Science Center at the University of California, Berkley,

> Mindfulness means maintaining a moment-by-moment awareness of our

---

[10] Pavi Sandhu (2015), Retrieved from https://blogs.scientificamerican.com.

thoughts, feelings, bodily sensations, and surrounding environment, through a gentle, nurturing lens. Mindfulness also involves acceptance, meaning that we pay attention to our thoughts and feelings without judging them—without believing, for instance, that there's a "right" or "wrong" way to think or feel in a given moment. When we practice mindfulness, our thoughts tune into what we're sensing in the present moment rather than rehashing the past or imagining the future.

Though it has its roots in Buddhist meditation, the secular practice of mindfulness has entered the American mainstream in recent years, in part through the work of Jon Kabat-Zinn and his Mindfulness-Based Stress Reduction (MBSR) program, which he launched at the University of Massachusetts Medical School in 1979.[11]

As one reads the article, there is further encouragement to ask, "Why practice it (mindfulness), and How do I cultivate it?"

If God's word is truth and John 14:26 tells us that the Holy Spirit teaches us *all* things, then why would we immerse ourselves in a godless ceremony? Why would we not judge our emotions, thoughts, or feelings as they come our way?

---

[11] https://greatergood.berkeley.edu/topic/mindfulness/definition.

We are called to discern the spirits (1 John 4:1–3). Romans 12:2 instructs us, "Do not be conformed to this world…test and approve what is the will of God."

You may use any incantation you desire to *prove* that mindfulness is of God and therefore Christian, but in reality, anyone who communicates this is clearly deluded. Why then are we attending seminaries to receive training and certification in disciplines which are clearly in contradiction to the word of God? These teachings must not make their way back to local churches or into God-centered counseling sessions.

If then psychotherapy was birthed by these two atheistic fathers, Breuer and Freud, it may be clearly affirmed that psychotherapy is not of God. What is not of God is contrary to God. What is not of God should not appear in Christian educational institutions. What is not of God should not be imposed upon His children. What is not of God is not for any biblically based counselor.

So why move away from Christian Counseling and psychotherapy? Are there no values and ideologies within Christian Counseling associations that offer 'Christian' support to people who possess psychological obstacles? According to this author, if Christian counseling truly existed, where Jesus was preeminent in every counseling session, there would not be a need for the move away from Christian counseling. The term *Christian counseling* has been selected by organizations to give the appearance of being Christian. While they consider themselves to be Christian in worldview, these organizations are not purely Christian due to their use of secular psychotherapy. (YOU CAN BE CHRISTIAN BY BELIEF YET ATHEISTIC OR PAGAN BY PRACTICE.)

Jesus and His ability to heal the brokenhearted must be revealed in all sessions. In Luke 4:18, *"The Spirit of the*

CHRISTIANITY AND THE LAW OF SEPARATION

Lord is upon me, because he has anointed me to proclaim good news to the poor. He has sent me to proclaim release to the captives and the regaining of sight to the blind, to set free those who are oppressed."[12] Psychotherapy does not give time or space to Jesus. Remember, psychotherapy was developed by atheists. For this writer to follow the word of God, he must separate himself from Christian counseling groups that incorporate psychotherapy and which may not preach Jesus.

In the fall of 2013, the author of this book audited a seminary class entitled, "The Integration of Psychology and Religion." Due to ongoing counseling practice and the holding of membership within a Christian counseling/psychotherapist organization, it was critical to understand the potential alliance of these two disciplines, psychology and religion. In this class, religion and Christianity were synonymous terms. While studying the course material, it was not apparent within the classroom setting that the integration of the two subjects was not possible nor were the two subject matters considered incompatible. As the course unfolded, the classroom teaching developed and promoted the conviction for the full integration of psychology and Christianity. Integration in this context was the harmonization of philosophies between secular psychotherapy and Christian beliefs.

As this assimilation was being considered, there was an immediate focus on worldviews, worldly philosophy, and models of integration. It must be noted that the aforementioned seminary additionally teaches classes on the Freudian-inspired topics of psychological assessment and psychology of emotion while providing accredited degrees in counseling

---

[12] *New English Translation Bible*, Full Notes Edition (Thomas Nelson, 1996).

psychology. Theories of man and the world have crept into this author's Christian counseling organization through the auspices of higher education. Why would anyone continue to carry membership in an organization that embraces the concepts of man? Integration between ideas of man and the wisdom of God is not possible.

After spending hours in the classroom, it was obvious that the integration of psychology and Christianity is a valued theme within certified Christian counseling. When a Christian counselor embraces secular psychotherapy within his/her practice, additional monies, through clients and referrals, will flow in their direction. Furthermore, secular themes within psychotherapy provide the opportunity for the Christian counselor to avoid the topics of sin, repentance, and the need for a savior. For any counselor who values the principles of God, sin, repentance, and Jesus must be discussed with the counselee.

It is deeply concerning to see seminaries teaching theories that clearly contradict the word of God. While studying these worldviews, philosophies, and models of integration, the Holy Spirit impressed upon this author that though taught in a Christian seminary, these topics were not God-inspired principles. While viewing these concerns in hindsight, it is unfortunate for this author to have waited this long to move away from his Christian counseling association which incorporates psychologically inspired teaching. When this paper is read by concerned Christians, all will know why any counselor should flee Christian counseling organizations which are immersed in and integrated with secular psychotherapy.

Having now considered integration, which is at the heart of Christian counseling, it is the view of this writer that psychology, as a thesis of man, will never integrate, synthesize, and synchronize with the wisdom and word of God. It is within this statement that biblically based counseling demonstrates why it will never adopt this worldly philosophy of counseling. Assimilation of God's wisdom and man's wisdom is not possible.

The hypothesis of perceived integration, psychology being aligned with Christianity in itself, pulls us away from the heart of God. As stated, the attempt to integrate the wisdom of man with the wisdom of God is not possible. There is not any other choice for biblical counselors and this author than to hold to a nonintegrationist posture. The amalgamation of psychology and Christianity is contrary to the word of God. We must not associate with nor support any organization which does not exclusively teach the word of God. The sufficiency and teachings of scripture are the main characteristics of the biblically based counselor.

Isaiah 55:8–9 reminds us that God's thoughts are so much greater than our thoughts. Integration of religion and psychology is the marginalization of the thoughts, words, and wisdom of God the creator. Colossians 2:8 warns us that the philosophy of man will cheat and deceive us. As we consider counseling God's way, we immediately know that man's way of counseling must never be considered a component of biblically based counseling. God is holy; man is not. Man and secular psychotherapy cannot contend with the wisdom of God.

Second Peter 1:3 tells us that everything we require to live a godly life is contained in the words and wisdom of God. As we look at the world around us and the evil which persists, we are reminded that the end of this age will eventually come. Portions of scripture such as Matthew 24, Jude,

2 Peter 2, and 2 Thessalonians 2 speak to a great falling away and end-time deception which will occur. Man's wisdom as it attempts to intersect with God's wisdom will actually lead many people into the realm of being deceived.

As people of God, we must never allow our false perceptions to distract disciples from the truth of God's word. We must align ourselves with biblically based counselors because the mutual belief states that integration between God and man in the context of counseling is not possible. Secular psychotherapy does not align itself with the word of God nor with the true Christian counselor.

THE AUTHORITY OF SCRIPTURE

We might commence this discussion by viewing Deuteronomy 4:2. The word of God carries with it power and authority. As a result, we see here in Deuteronomy that we are not to add or subtract from its pages. The authority is complete; we are to accept the commands as given to us in the scriptures. Jesus reiterates this in Matthew 5:18; until heaven and earth pass away, the authority of God and the words and grammar of the Bible will not pass away. The word of God and its authority will stand forever.

Jeremiah is told by God to write down everything told to him because it is the authority of God by which Jeremiah prophesied (Jeremiah 30:2).

Moses called the word of God the law of God and the witness from God against man (Deuteronomy 31:25–26).

In the high priestly prayer of John 17, Jesus says to the Father that all God has given to the Son, He (Jesus) has passed on this authority to the disciples. Furthermore, the apostle Paul in 1 Corinthians 14:37 makes the bold claim that what he has written are the commands of God.

Psalm 119:160 tells us that the entirety of God's word is truth. God's judgments and His authority live forever.

In the following unit on inspiration, we will view 2 Timothy 3:16–17; these verses talk about the authority of God's word to correct and instruct. These instructions equip a Christian for every good work.

Finally, Matthew 4:4 shows us that the word of God will sustain men and women. It is the authority of God by which we live our lives.

The Inspiration of Scripture

Inspiration, with respect to scripture, is the understanding that God had directed men to write down His decrees and commandments. As God moved upon men with the working of the Holy Spirit, His words were spiritually disclosed and then placed into written form by these select human authors. Men were spiritually trained and influenced by God to write down God's words. There was obvious interaction between God and each individual author. God's words to men were so distinct and inspired that we believe the sixty-six books of the Bible to have come directly from God.

The canon of scripture is not merely the words of men but, first and foremost, the words of God. These words were superintended by the Holy Spirit. Inspiration in reality is taking the spiritual word of God and placing it into human form. Paul claims in 2 Corinthians 2: 13 that the things written down are from the Holy Spirit.

All scripture is given by God. We see in 2 Timothy 3:16–17 that all scripture is given with inspiration and vision by God and is profitable. The Greek word in 2 Timothy 3:16 is *theopneustos*; it is God breathed. God was so intimate with the authors of the Bible that He breathed into them His words. As the authors were moved by God, they wrote His words.

Hebrews 1:1 tells us that God spoke to men at various times and in various ways. God has spoken to us through the prophets and spoken to us by His Son. Second Peter 1:20–21 states unequivocally that God has inspired all things including the writing of His words and prophetic utterances. Humans were moved by the Holy Spirit to speak and write the ordinances of God. John 14:26 tells us that the Holy Spirit will teach us all things and bring to mind the inspired word of God. Second Peter 1:3–4 talks about God's divine power giving us all things which allow us to have the victorious Christian life. This includes the exceedingly great and precious promises in His divinely inspired Bible.

Finally, we need to consider Exodus 20:1, "God spoke." While vital in approach, we know that God provided inspired words to Moses. From these words, we as Christians receive morality and ethics through the Ten Commandments. God's inspiration for man has given us clear insight into how we are to function within and influence society.

BIBLICAL INERRANCY

The Bible is without error. It is without mistake or fault. First and foremost, we claim it is without error because we believe it is the word of God. God would never supply us with a document that is false or incorrect.

In its original languages of Hebrew, Aramaic, and Greek, the Bible is accurate to God's inspired words. Accurate translations, therefore, are of extreme importance. As much as is humanly possible, translators are required to be accurate to the original words, intent, and context of the original manuscripts. The Bible is without mistake or fault in all of its original teachings. Because the Bible is God breathed as viewed in 2 Timothy 3:16, we know there are not any errors contained in its pages.

First Corinthians 2:13 states that the Holy Spirit teaches on a spiritual-to-spiritual level. By stating this, the apostle Paul is claiming the accuracy of God's word. When we speak to the accuracy of the word of God, we speak of the correctness and truth of His word. We have titled God's precise and accurate word to man, the Bible.

Examples of God-inspired words are scattered throughout the Bible. Deuteronomy 18 gives us a glimpse of a new prophet such as Moses. God was going to provide this new prophet (Jesus, Messiah) with His words to speak to the nations. When we consider inspired words and the Bible as God-inspired words, we know there is not any error. Jeremiah 1:9 is a promise to Jeremiah that God will deliver to Jeremiah His (God's) words. These words are always without error. These words are written without error for our edification.

When we consider inerrancy, this does not mean that we are overlooking poor translation(s). Therefore, when we possess and use accurate translations, we can attest to the fact that the Bible does not contain myth or fantasy. Inerrancy includes the notion of trustworthiness, hence the need for accurate translations to be used in our daily lives and in the teaching of the word of God.

Psalm 119:11 says that we memorize scripture as it will be faithful to keep us from sin. This is trustworthiness at the core of inerrancy. God's inerrant, infallible word, the Bible, will keep us on the path of sanctification. Infallibility refers to the trustworthiness and accuracy of scripture. The Bible will not lead us into error. When we view this in light of who God is, truth tells us that the Bible is without myth or fantasy. John 17:17 reminds us that God's word is truth. It is perfect.

SUFFICIENCY OF SCRIPTURE

In a biblical counseling setting, scripture is the only element counselors require to see transformation in peoples' lives. There is not any other book by which we need to explain the Christian experience to counselees. Although there are resources other than the Bible which will be recommended to counselees, scripture is the base for all counseling discussions. The Bible is adequate, it is accurate, and it will not lead man astray.

Scripture gives us the meaning of life. Scripture gives us the word of God. Scripture reminds us of the commandments of God and the fact that we are to keep God's commandments. Every aspect of societal living is explained from the perspective of God through the Bible. We receive a clear understanding of God, His nature, and His attributes from scripture. John 20:30–31 says that if we read God's word, we will see the principles and teachings of Jesus within its pages.

Our knowledge of God is revealed to us through scripture. This is why scripture and scripture only is recognized within Christianity. The doctrine of *sola scriptura* (scripture alone) says that the Bible is the only infallible source of authority and truth for the Christian disciples.

CHRISTIANITY AND THE LAW OF SEPARATION

Isaiah 9:6 encourages us to know that Jesus is the wonderful counselor. It is by the leading of the Holy Spirit and the usage of scripture in the counseling session that counselors find their strength. Because Jesus gives us His wisdom through the Bible, this one book is sufficient for the ills of mankind. Counsel is found deep within the pages of the scriptures.

Psalm 19:7–9 speaks to the impact scripture has on human beings. The law of God converts the soul, it makes the heart rejoice, and it brings truth and righteousness to all who read the words. In fact, verse 10 tells us that the words of God are more precious than the finest piece of gold.

Psalm 119:105 talks about God's word lighting our path. God's testimonies are wonderful; they are breathed to us (Psalm 119:129). We teach from the Bible only as it brings life into the world.

AS INERRANCY SPEAKS TO THE RULE OF FAITH, SO SUFFICIENCY SPEAKS TO THE RULE OF PRACTICE

Inerrancy is the accuracy of God's word and therefore the accuracy of all the claims of Christianity. Any rule of faith dictates a set of beliefs that causes religion to exist. Within the rule(s) of faith exists the confidence in any religious system. For the Christian community, our theological standards and beliefs come from the divine word of God, the inerrant word of God. We also have the Holy Spirit as a comforter, teacher, and guide (John 14:26). The Holy Spirit leads us into all truth and demonstrates the inerrancy of scripture. It is, however, in the interpretation of the divine word where sometimes the accurate rules and truth of Christianity are subjugated. For the biblically based counselor, the Holy Spirit must lead and guide the counseling process.

Inerrancy, as it speaks to the rule of faith, dictates to the Christian community Christianity's set of values and rules. Therefore, the interpretation of this truthful document, the Bible, is vital for Christian living. The authority of Christianity comes from the fact that the Bible is without error or fault. The accuracy of the Bible, then, is placed in front of the Christian community; and the individual Christian, the rule of faith.

God's divine power gives us all things that pertain to life and godliness (2 Peter 1:3). Sufficiency of the authority of God's word is this guarantee. As we use the word of God in daily living and counseling settings, scripture is all that is required for spiritual transformation. The Bible in and of itself is the most competent tool available to the biblical counselor. We are putting into practice as it were the rules and standards of faith which we have gleaned from the inerrant word of God.

God's word is the source of our active faith. Second Peter 1:3 is practical in nature; all we need for life and godliness is found in the all-sufficiency of the word of God. Second Timothy 3:16–17 instructs us to know that the God-breathed Bible is there for doctrine correction and daily living. Sufficiency, the adequacy of the Bible, then dictates our practice and how we live our Christian experience. Sufficiency allows us to be continually sanctified and not shaken in mind or spirit (2 Thessalonians 2:2). We ask, "What is God's standard for man? And by what practice do we accomplish this standard?" The rule of God is the word of God.

GENERAL AND SPECIAL REVELATION, AS IT REVEALS THE MAJESTY OF GOD, WITHIN THE COUNSELING PROCESS

General revelation is available to all people. This revelation would be viewed as nature displaying the majesty of God (Psalm 104:1), teaching from the word of God (Ephesians 4:11), and philosophical debate occurring after the study of God's word (1 Peter 3:15–16). Psalm 19 exclaims that the heavens are witnessing to man the glory of God. We must stop with this premise and go no further. As stated below, the sciences should not be used to further unpack general revelation. Furthermore, animistic debate, referring to everything in nature possessing a soul and thus possessing a certain *revelation*, does not belong within Christianity or the general revelation of God.

Special revelation has been defined in several ways. While all revelation from God is supernatural, special revelation is beyond normal expectations of revelation. Hebrews 1:1 says that God spoke at specific times and in specific ways to the fathers and prophets. These times were special and out of the ordinary. Therefore, special revelation is God revealing Himself to us through His word. Special revelation takes precedence over general revelation.

For biblical counseling purposes, general revelation must never wander into the area of the natural sciences (physics, biology, chemistry), unless the natural sciences confirm what general revelation has already revealed. Additionally, we must use the word of God as a special revelation in counseling. We do not use the discussion of the natural sciences as the explanation for God's creation. It is the word of God that discloses nature and the majesty of God to the counselee. As we experience nature, it is the Holy Spirit who discloses God to us (John 14:26). Hence, God reveals God.

General revelation will not contradict special revelation. The general understanding of God and His creation will be applied through the lens of scripture, God's special revelation to man. When in a counseling setting, we practically apply the word of God to the Christian walk. General revelation becomes important as this revelation points fallen man toward a Holy God. Creation is broken and fragile because of the fall of man.

There is a need for reconciliation to occur between God and man. If we hear the word, we must become doers of the word (James 1:23–24). We approach God through general revelation as being taught through special revelation, knowing that creation is broken. The word of God is our truth and authority. Jesus is named as our propitiation (1 John 4:10) and reconciles fallen man to God the creator.

Special revelation then becomes dominant over general revelation in biblical counseling. Special revelation is the known truth revealed through the scripture. Special revelation is the revelation of salvation and spiritual healing.

Through special revelation, the word of God, men receive insight regarding the commandments of God. Furthermore, special revelation gives us insight into how the commandments of God are to be applied to our lives. Romans 10:17 speaks to faith coming from hearing and hearing by the word (special revelation) of God. Matthew 4:4 instructs us, in counseling, that every piece of special revelation comes from the mouth of God. Therefore, the sufficiency of scripture is of extreme importance for the biblical counselor.

FIVE INFLUENTIAL COUNSELING BOOKS TO CONSIDER

Although this author has carefully read several books and textbooks regarding *Christian* counseling, these five books resonate well within the context of true Bible-based counseling. Each of these five books has had a profound impact on my thought process because of the consideration of psychotherapy and non-Biblical theories which have been incorporated into Christian counseling. These texts wrap themselves with biblical annotations, not the theories of man.

1. *Theology of Biblical Counseling: The Doctrinal Foundations of Counseling Ministry,* by Heath Lambert

Heath Lambert's initial assertion that counseling is a theological discipline bodes well with the heart of God. God wishes for all men to be saved and wishes for all men to be true followers of Jesus Christ. Within this assertion is Lambert's belief that Christianity and psychotherapy do not align. Although everything of Jesus would support those who are in the counseling arena through belief in the atonement, righteousness, and sanctification, we know that secular psychotherapy is not able to support a true God-centered counseling relationship.

It is encouraging to see Lambert's historical recollection of how psychotherapy crept into Christian counseling. As we consider this "creeping in," we realize that God did not intend for the integration of psychology with Christianity. With this consideration in mind, leaving psychotherapy-based counseling and stepping into the world of biblically based counseling are essential for the Christian community. God has always said that Jesus is enough. Lambert speaks about the sufficiency of Scripture and the doctrine of Scripture. Lambert leads the reader into the thought of Jesus being enough, through the knowledge that God's wisdom far exceeds the secular wisdom of man.

Near the end of the text, there is a section on influential writing. Lambert is clear, in appendix "A," page 321 that a biblically based model of counseling is far healthier than a secular, psychotherapy model of counseling. God deals with the heart of man; secular psychotherapy neglects to address the spiritual void in mankind. This is a great book to consider for the person wishing to move into biblical-based counseling. This book provides further insights into the things of God.

2. *The Christian Counselor's Manual*, by Jay E. Adams

Dr. Jay Adams is considered to be the pioneer in the area of biblically based nouthetic counseling. Each reading of his text will influence the reader to consider whether or not psychotherapy belongs in Christian counseling. The conclusion, to the inquiry, states unequivocally that psychotherapy does not belong in biblical counseling.

Nouthetic is derived from the Greek word *nouthesia*. This term calls all Christians to admonish and give direction to fellow Christians within the context of the Christian community. As we consider truth within the community, God's approach to counseling must exist; therefore, counseling God's way is the only way. Dr. Jay Adams influences this reader toward this standard of belief. While there may be different persuasions of theology within the text (e.g., Calvinism versus Arminianism), Adams's claim to the belief of Jesus and Jesus only for counseling is valid.

As Christians navigate their lives within the broken, fallen world, we are commanded to follow the precepts of God. Adams reminded this reader that the ongoing work of sanctification is the key component to living a victorious Christian life. Adams contends and persuades many readers to know that theological and biblical training is the only requirement for healthy, biblically based counseling. When we view counseling through God's eyes and not the viewpoint of man, we understand God's love and care for humanity.

3. *How to Counsel God's Way*, by Bob Hoekstra

As with the authors already referenced, Bob Hoekstra is adamant about the fact that psychotherapy should never mix with biblically based counseling. This statement regarding Hoekstra's core belief is influential enough for readers to ponder a move away from psychotherapy and into God's way of counseling.

John 17:17 tells us that God's Word is truth. Hoekstra holds to this principle while also claiming that Jesus and the gospel are enough for the evils of society. It is always through the discipleship process that we as Christians are able to influence and be influenced by Jesus Christ. Hoekstra is a huge encouragement as we ponder our lives as disciples of Jesus Christ.

Hoekstra further encourages us to remember that we should not get "bogged down" in sidebar issues within the context of counseling. These sidebar issues distract from the truth and message of Jesus Christ. As biblical counselors, we must stay on task and direct the focus of counselees onto the life of Jesus Christ. The Holy Spirit, the Word of God, and Jesus's example are all we need to live a life of godly enjoyment.

Hoekstra reminds all readers that psychological counseling only modifies and, at times, manipulates a person's behavior. The ongoing work of God's sanctifying grace is what profoundly changes people into God-fearing individuals. We speak to counselees with the love of Christ. The Holy Spirit speaks to counselees regarding their need to correct their lives. Hoekstra says that we always move the counselee toward a godly solution for the hurts of the world.

4. *Instruments in the Redeemer's Hands: People in Need of Change Helping People in Need of Change, by Paul David Tripp*

Paul David Tripp writes this book from the perspective of biblical counselors serving the body of Christ. God uses us as He wishes to use us. As vessels of the Most-High God, we must be willing and active members of the body of Christ. Tripp reminded me that my responsibility is to be a servant of God and minister the love of Jesus Christ. As consideration is given to the world of biblical counseling, we must direct counselees back to the gospel of Jesus.

Our main purpose in life is to glorify God. Secular psychotherapy suggests that our main purpose in life is understood within a wide selection of ideas on a continuum of worldly desires. Tripp causes all readers to know that Jesus Christ gives us a God-ordained purpose. Things of the world must pass away (2 Corinthians 5:17). As the Holy Spirit directs a yielded life, healing and inner peace will be discovered.

Tripp contends with factual accuracy the need to know that Scripture has the answers for the world's issues. Tripp cautioned me to not wander away from the truth and illuminating presence of God's Word. As we hide God's Word in our hearts (Psalm 119:11), we will have less tendency to sin against the commands of God. As biblically based counselors, we must establish this knowledge in the hearts and minds of counselees. Of course, this installation is by the leading of the Holy Spirit. Tripp's influence on me is directly related to my need to be a devoted member of the bride of Christ.

5. *Curing the Heart: A Model for Biblical Counseling, by Howard A. Eyrich and William L. Hines*

Howard Eyrich and William Hines commence their work with the claim that the Bible is all we need to counsel God's way. The authors spoke to this author in a very profound manner regarding the presence of God in the context of counseling. They state that the Bible is the foundation for our lives as disciples of Jesus Christ. While we may have always believed this fact, we now move our lives and counseling practices away from psychotherapy and into the illumination of God's word. All we need for us to speak godly living into the lives of counselees is the Word of God, because of it being illuminated by the Holy Spirit.

The authors talk about general and special revelation as it relates to God the Father. God is constantly revealing who He is into broken mankind. It is through revelation that men and women see God as the creator and see the need for sinful men to be reconciled to this creator. It is by the shed blood of Jesus Christ that man is reconciled to God. Jesus as our propitiation has linked us back to God. There is an opportunity for true regeneration to take place in anyone who is willing to accept regeneration through the shed blood of Christ. As counselors, we are joyfully obligated to share these truths with counselees.

Eyrich and Hines encourage us to understand that the Word of God is not a tool of destruction. Instead, God's word brings life and spiritual health while bringing truth into a dark world. God's Word is a book of comfort. God's Word is a book of love, and it brings all people to the realization that God has good intentions for the human race.

Howard Eyrich and William Hines provide additional, practical administrative details for counselors. Whether we consider the stages of counseling relationships or the requirement for detailed files on counselees, the authors provide essential details on counseling matters.

DISCIPLES OF JESUS CHRIST SHOULD NOT MAKE THE CLAIM "YOU CANNOT REALLY LOVE GOD UNLESS YOU LOVE YOURSELF"

This statement does not belong in the vocabulary of any disciple of Jesus Christ. Within this statement, there appears to be the notion that love for ourselves will come before our love for God. As biblical counselors, we always want to rely on the wisdom and love of God. When we place ourselves in front of God's desires for His creation, by claiming love for ourselves, spiritual healing will become impossible. Romans 5:8 speaks to God loving us while we were still in a state of perpetual sin. God's love appeared within creation before we had the opportunity to love God in a reciprocal manner. We love God and God alone. Self-love cannot exist. We truly are able to love God without regard for self-love.

Genesis 1:26 makes the bold claim that we are created in the image of God. When we allow this thought to sink into our souls, we immediately realize that self-love is contrary to the nature of God. However, the fall of man in Genesis 3 speaks to the separation between a perfect God with perfect love and now an imperfect man. Ephesians 4: 22 cautions us to hate the old, fallen man because this nature is contrary to God's nature. We were created by God to worship Him and worship Him alone. When self-love is placed in a counseling setting, we move away from the perfect love of God the Father and into a love formulated by the world. His perfect love has been placed upon His creation.

Second Timothy 3:1–5 cautions all of us to know that in the last days, men will become lovers of themselves. This self-love scheme is contrary to God's desire for mankind, for His creation. If this caution is given to the church, we must obey. Obedience in this sense is staying away from the delusion of self-love. Self-love is imperfect love. Self-love is self-focus. Self-love is what occurred in the Garden of Eden.

In Genesis 3:5, we see the notion of Eve, operating in human form, wanting to be like God. She was promised that if she ate, her eyes would be open, thereby knowing good and evil. As Eve considered this, she realized that the tree was pleasant to the eyes. She was seduced by the concept of being like God. Eve's self-love, her desire to be like God, was the driver which caused her to sin. Due to the sinful nature of Adam and Eve, Genesis 3:22–23 shows how God banished them from the garden as they now knew good and evil. Self-love was the catalyst to wanting to be like God and thereby allowing sin to enter the human race.

Self-love is taught within the four walls of societal bliss. Society claims that as we love ourselves for who we are, we are then able to love others. The deception in the Garden of Eden also possessed this base thought process. Matthew 16:24 is Jesus's claim to deny ourselves, take up our cross, and follow Him. Self-love is a reliance on us to love with imperfect love. If we truly wish to allow Jesus to be Lord, then we love Him and allow Him to concern Himself with our well-being. In fact, 1 John 3:11 and 1 John 4:7–8 say we should love others. There is not any mention of loving ourselves. When Jesus is Lord, we love Him, and then we love those around us.

Second Corinthians 5:17 says that if we are in Christ, old things have passed away. Old things include the corrupted, self-seeking manner in which we live. Love for our own well-being interferes with God's plan for His creation.

THE SOVEREIGNTY OF GOD AND ITS IMPORTANCE TO THE COUNSELING PROCESS

By definition, the sovereignty of God means that He has the authority over all matters and is the final decision-maker with respect to the future of man. Although the world appears to be chaotic in nature, God wills and purposes His good will for mankind. Philippians 2:13 states that God works in us. Colossians 1:16 says that God created all things for His glory. Due to God being the creator, He is positioned to look after His creation. God has the ultimate authority to rule over His created order.

There is not anything that takes place within the world where God's influence is not known. God is in control. Psalm 103:19 claims that God has established His throne in heaven, and He is the supreme ruler of all. In order to be the supreme ruler, He is regarded as the supreme sovereign. Therefore, God is autonomous in His decision-making processes and has full authority to make these decisions.

Counselees may be struggling with the notion that God is in charge of His creation. Evil, wars, famines, and the like exist. At times, it appears as though God is not in control of His creation. However, we must always look at the sovereignty of God with the end in mind. In the end, Jesus does return, and He sets up His kingdom and eventually judges all mankind. There is comfort for the counselee with this thought. Revelation 21:6 says that God is the beginning and the end. As disciples of Jesus Christ, we trust Him, and we trust God the Father. Romans 8:28 says that all things work out for the good of mankind. God has instilled His decision-making process into the actions of mankind.

God provides for His children. In light of this, we know that God has given us the wisdom to make decisions that ultimately influence the end results. Godly wisdom and the leading of the Holy Spirit, if accurately discerned and followed, place the child of God into the will of God. Within the context of Romans 8, we perceive that God has provided for us a portion of His wisdom, which aids in His will being fulfilled. When God instills His decision-making processes into our lives, His sovereignty is manifested. So within His sovereignty, God allows free will, knowing that all things will work for His good.

God allows kings to rise and fall, He allows famines to take place, and He will allow Jesus to judge the nations (Matthew 25:31–46). Colossians 1:13–16 makes the claim that God has delivered us from the darkness. We are His creation, and through Him, all decisions for His creation are and will be made. So when a counselee comes to us in distress, whether it is the future or even fear of the coronavirus, as biblical counselors, we direct them to Scripture which proves that God is in control.

Although God is in command, as counselors, we encourage counselees to pray. Second Chronicles 7:14 is a verse that shows that prayer is used as a confession. If we humble ourselves and pray, God will heal our sinful state. First Chronicles 4:10 shows where prayer is used as a form of petitioning the Holy God. At the end of this verse, we see that God heard Jabez's prayer and granted His request. Acts 12:1–11 is an example of where corporate prayer, engaged by a local body of believers, turned out for the release of Peter from prison. God is in control, but we teach prayer as the opportunity for counselees to be involved in the work of God.

God knows all things. God sees all things. God plans all things. Romans 11:33–36 is a huge encouragement for all including the counselee. The wisdom and knowledge of God are insurmountable. To God alone, all things are submissive. Through God, all things were created, and all things will come to pass according to His good pleasure.

SOVEREIGNTY OF GOD AND FREE WILL OF MAN

We must always think of the sovereignty of God with the end in mind. While we perceive chaos in the world, we know that Jesus will return, defeat Satan, and set up His millennial kingdom. (Revelation 20:1–6). So while we question the turmoil in the world, we understand that the one true God has the plan in place to see His decrees and His prophecies fulfilled. God's ultimate blueprint for mankind will be fulfilled by Him.

Does God allow man to make free will decisions? Absolutely. Because we are created in the image of God (Genesis 1:26), we must possess free will. After all, the God we worship and know to be the one true God is the epitome of free will. God allowed Satan to make the decision to rebel (Isaiah 14). God allowed Judas to betray Jesus (John 18). God grants us the decision to either believe in Jesus or reject Jesus (John 3:16–21).

When we counsel, we must pay attention to the fact that counselees have made some poor choices. By their own free will, counselees may have sinned against the decrees of the Holy God. It is through these negative choices that counselees need to be challenged in dealing with sin issues. James 4:7 states that if we submit to God, Satan will flee. Free will is engaged in this decision. We need to have the mindset to resist Satan; this is free will in action. Second Corinthians 10:5 instructs us to take every thought captive. Free will thinkers have the ability to obey or disobey. While the Holy Spirit has been given to us as a guide (John 14:26), God does not manipulate us into submission and obedience. He will, however, chastise and correct us (Proverbs 3:11–12). When our free will interferes with the will of God, He will correct us.

DEFINING THE PROVIDENCE OF GOD AND ITS IMPORTANCE IN THE COUNSELING PROCESS

It is with great joy that as biblically based counselors, we are able to present to counselees the knowledge that God will supply all their needs. God will provide for these individuals what is required so as to be sustained in their spiritual and physical settings. We see this promise in Philippians 4:19. When we speak about the providence of God, there is a connotation that God provides all things as needed for all people and for His creation. God's providence is considered to be one of His attributes. As an attribute, divine intervention for man is intrinsic to the character of the Holy God. There is a further understanding that when we speak about the providence of God, we are referring to God's intervention in the whole of the universe.

As we consider the providence of the Holy God, we are speaking specifically about His providing for our needs. God determines for us what is necessary for our sustenance. While we may think we *need* things in our life so as to feel fulfilled, we know that God has the direct knowledge of what we need in order to be sustained. There are many instances in the

Bible where the providence of God is noted. These portions of Scripture are a great resource for the context of biblical counseling—counseling God's way.

Genesis 22:8 is an example where Abraham says to his son Isaac that God will provide. Abraham's faith in God to provide was realized in Genesis 22:13. In Genesis 22:14, as a tribute to the one true God, Abraham called the place of sacrifice. "The Lord Will Provide."

Matthew 10:27–31 is a further example of the providence of God. We are told to go and make disciples. When we "go," the Holy Spirit will go with us. God's care over us causes us to not fear man. God's care over us says that if God concerns Himself with a sparrow falling to the ground, how much more will He care for us as humans? As we teach the providence of God to counselees, we pray that their fears will be alleviated.

God has control over His creation. We reviewed this in the previous section when speaking to the sovereignty of God. As we counsel from a biblical perspective, we teach this aspect of the character of God. Because God has control over His creation, He has the ability to supply all our needs. First Kings 17:4 says that God directed the ravens to feed Elijah. In 1 Kings 18:38, the fire of God fell and consumed the sacrifice. We see in the book of Jonah chapter 4 where God appointed His creation to act on His behalf. In Mark 4, we take note of how the sea and wind obey almighty God. God is omnipotent, omnipresent, and omniscient. By these words, we know that God provides all things as needed. We provide this knowledge through the leading of the Holy Spirit into the lives of counselees.

DEFINING THE JUSTICE OF GOD

We will commence this discussion by referring to Proverbs 24:12. In this verse resides the indication that men are pleading willful ignorance in the face of committing wrongful acts. God says that regardless of outward appearance, He judges the heart of men and renders judgment accordingly. God's justice places upon men the need to be consecrated to our God. Without men being dedicated to the ordinances of God, it is impossible to please God. Hebrews 11:6 commands us to come to God in faith as those who diligently seek Him and thereby receive our just reward.

God's justice must be defined by His holiness. Because He is holy, He will not tolerate any amount of sin or wrongdoing. As we bring out this fact in a counseling session, we are encouraging the counselee to know that sin in their lives needs to be exposed. When sin is exposed, it will be dealt with through the leading of the Holy Spirit. When we sit with counselees, we are encouraging them to be disciples of Jesus Christ. Discipleship is defined as being slaves of Jesus. Justice then incorporates the belief that sin does not persist in the lives of Jesus's disciples, hence the need to expose sin. First Peter 1:15–16 claims that the one who is holy calls us to be holy. Righteousness is available for all. Counselees must understand that in order to receive spiritual healing, they must have the righteousness of God imputed upon their regenerated lives.

God's justice dictates and defines the fact that He is perfectly righteous. God is without fault nor is He capable of committing evil. Because of His perfection, He is obligated to judge the hearts and intentions of all men at a level that He has determined. His justice is the imposition of righteous laws and righteous outcomes upon His creation. Because of the fall of man, righteousness, which was originally placed into man, was immediately unavailable. It was unavailable in the sense that man could no longer possess an immediacy to this righteousness.

For any of us to now approach a Holy God, we are required to have a sacrifice in place. Due to the justice of God, He must be appeased. Hebrews 9:22 claims that without the shedding of blood, there is not any remission of sin. Jesus came to earth to shed His blood for mankind. When the counselee realizes the extent of the sacrifice, they will know that a Holy God has put in place a righteous act of reconciliation. God's justice needed to have a link between His holiness and unholy man. It is Jesus who acted as this link. He is our propitiation. First John 2:2 says that Jesus is the propitiation, the link between Holy God and unholy man. God's mercy now is put in place. Because of the righteous act of Jesus dying on the cross, God's justice is satisfied. His mercy states that He keeps from us the punishment we deserve.

We do know that God holds us accountable for our actions. This must be emphasized with counselees. Even though His righteousness is imputed upon regenerated individuals, we still are responsible for our actions. If we deny sin in our lives, we are deceiving ourselves. We see this fact in 1 John 1:8. If we confess these sins, Holy God will forgive us and cleanse us (1 John 1:9). When we deal with our sins, God's justice and portions of His holiness are understood.

As we consider the justice of God, we realize that it is God alone who possesses the responsibility to mete out justice. For those counselees who have been brutally mistreated by others, we are able to direct them to the word of God. Deuteronomy 32:35 and Romans 12:19 tell us that vengeance is an act of a Holy God. God will repay those who serve injustices to others. For the counselee, forgiveness is paramount. It is never our right or responsibility to ensure that justice is served against another human. In order for the counselee to move forward, they must forgive and allow God to deal with the offender.

DEFINING THE LOVE OF GOD

Love is an attribute of our Heavenly Father. Romans 5:8 tells us that while we were yet sinners, Christ died for us. God loves us beyond our finite comprehension. When we accept Jesus as Savior, God's love is manifested in our lives. As counselors, we must demonstrate the fruit of the spirit. Love, joy, and peace must be present in the counseling relationship. When we pray for the counselee, we must ask the Holy Spirit to produce love in us. Love in us causes love to flow out of us and into the counseling relationship. As sin is revealed in the life of the counselee, we must express love. It is the love of God and the desire for sanctification that cause counselees to turn from their sin.

It is hard to define the love of God because of His majesty. God is so far above anything or anyone. Isaiah 55:8–9 gives us a glimpse into this belief. God's ways and thoughts are superior to man's ways. Man's love is defined on a smaller scale than God's love. Man's definition of love includes admiration, care, concern, and compassion for someone or something. There is a wide range of emotions involved in the defining of man's love including an awareness of deep affection.

CHRISTIANITY AND THE LAW OF SEPARATION

Man's definition is very inadequate regarding the love of God. In order to fully comprehend God's love, we will need to leave this broken world and gain entrance into heaven. Yet within a counseling session, showing the love of God to counselees is of extreme importance. In John 13:34–35, Jesus commands us to love one another. When we love, we show others that we are Christ's disciples. Although man's definition of love is inadequate, it will be our demonstration of care, concern, and compassion for the counselee, which will point them to the love of God. Although we are broken vessels, God will use us in the counseling context.

As we speak to counselees, we are actually encouraged by the thought of not being able to fully comprehend and explain God's love. If we could fully comprehend and define God's love, then He really would not be a God of infinite power and might. As we are led by the Holy Spirit, we will model the love of God to counselees.

We do realize that while we were yet sinners, God demonstrated His love and sent Jesus to die for the sins of the world (Romans 5:7–8). God's love is in action. We feel this love, His deep affection for us, by knowing that Jesus died for those who did not have fellowship with Him. The scripture 1 John 4:8 says that God in and of Himself is love. His essence, His being is love. We are not capable of disconnecting God, who He is as God, from His personal attribute of love.

God so loved the world that He gave His only Son (John 3:16). Throughout Psalm 136, we see that God's mercy endures forever. His mercy, keeping from us the punishment we deserve, is love in action. God's essence of love is demonstrated in Psalm 139. He knit us in our mothers' wombs. God loves us. He chastises and corrects those whom He loves (Proverbs 3:11–12). God wants the best for us, and that is why correction occurs. While correction hurts, it is God's love in action. He wants us to come to Him because everything we require for daily living is found in God.

Throughout the Bible, we see God's love in action. Because of this evidentiary reality, we should share the love of God with counselees. In Malachi 2:11, we see that God loves His holy institution. The nation of Israel had been unfaithful to this institution, that being complete and devoted worship of the one true God. God's love through His commandments stated that He wanted His people to return to this worship. It is within our worship of God that we are able to witness His love for us. God lives in and loves His people. We have passed from death to life when we love as God loves (1 John 3:14). Romans 8:39 makes a further claim that we cannot be separated from the love of God. As His disciples, God's presence is with us. First John 4:16 states that if we abide in God, we abide in love. First Corinthians 13:7 tells us that love hopes for all things. God is love. Because God is love, we speak to the counselee about the hope of a brighter future.

COUNSELING WITH THOSE WHO FEAR WORLD EVENTS

In 2 Timothy 2:6–7, the apostle Paul challenges his apprentice Timothy with regard to being a devoted disciple of Jesus Christ. Paul may have been concerned that Timothy was struggling with his ability to move forward with his Christian faith. In Greek, there is this analogy that to "stir up" the gift from God is to stir up the embers in a fire. In other words, Christians are not to allow our burning passion for God to die or go out. We are to stoke up the proverbial fire that God has placed into our hearts. When we stoke God's fire within us, fear is alleviated.

We are reminded that God has not given us a spirit of fear but power, love, and a sound mind. When Christians are fearful, it is not based on rational, sound biblical doctrine. Fear is not connected with the definition of the love of God. With all gentleness, I would challenge the thought process of this counselee. There is a need to understand this person's source of fear and encourage them to know that as God's children, we do not need to live in a state of fear. When fear is evident in a Christian, we may be witnessing a life lived in quiet desperation. John 10:10 reminds us that Jesus came to give us a victorious Christian life. Fear in any person does not allow for victory over Satan.

Fear is based on the unknown. When world events transpire, the person living in fear considers all possible contingencies concerning the outcomes of these events. Matthew 6:34 tells us to not worry about tomorrow. We are not to dwell on the *what-ifs* of world events. The *what-ifs* breed fear in our lives. As we read this verse, we are reminded that the present day in which we live has enough issues to keep us occupied. Fear of outcomes within world events is in truth a sin. It is disobedience to the command of not worrying about tomorrow.

When fear envelopes our thoughts, we are concentrating on ourselves and not on the God who created us and loves us. First John 4:18 tells us that there is no fear in love, especially God's love. Perfect love, which is only available from God, casts out all fear including mental torment. So as we consider this scenario, we would explore with the counselee the thoughts, Bible verses, and godly doctrine which have been documented within this answer. Furthermore, there is a need for biblically based counselors to pray with the counselee. As counselors, we desire to see the Holy Spirit complete a work of healing within the counselee. Prayer is the foundation of biblical counseling.

With regard to homework, I would ask the counselee to seek God with all his heart. We need to go to God when fear takes hold of our lives. We are able to ask the Holy God who loves us to reveal the source of fear in our lives. As we spend time in the presence of God, the Holy Spirit will reveal the truth to our hearts and minds. First Thessalonians 5:17 instructs all of us to pray without ceasing. When the source of fear is revealed, we will renounce the source and ask God to heal our thought processes.

There is also an encouragement for the counselee to mediate on the Word of God. Respectfully, there would be biblical reading assignments from 2 Corinthians 4:7–12 and 2 Corinthians 10:3–6. For the first portion of Scripture, the question would be, What does it mean to see fear press in against us, but yet through the leading of the Holy Spirit, we gain victory over fear? For the second portion of Scripture, the question to be addressed is this: What does it mean for fearful thoughts to be taken captive and with the help of the Holy Spirit to bring these thoughts into the obedience of Jesus Christ? As a final consideration, I would ask the counselee to search the Scriptures for the evidence of God taking fear out of the lives of those who have followed God.

IMPORTANCE OF JAMES 4:1–5 FOR MARITAL COUNSELING

Upon searching this portion of Scripture, it is obvious that it addresses selfish ambition, dissension, and discord. We know that as we study God's Word, to be a friend of this world means we are self-centered and an enemy of God. When we are an enemy of God, our marriage union suffers. Selfishness does not belong in a truly devoted disciple of Jesus. Therefore, selfishness does not belong in a godly marriage. Marital wars and fights occur when our worldly pleasures and ambitions supersede the will and love of God.

In chapter 3 of the book of James, we have noted that the disciples within the church at Jerusalem have followed earthly, devilish wisdom. Chapter 4 is a continuation of the caution to Christians to not follow this sensual, demonic wisdom. For the married couple, this is a pivotal moment within their marriage. For harmony to exist in a godly marriage, godly wisdom must be present. James 3:17 says that wisdom from above will bring purity and peace into the life of a disciple of Jesus Christ. When purity and peace exist in both spouses, who are led by the Holy Spirit, there is a promise that peace will exist in the marriage. James 4:1–5 is a caution to married couples to pay attention to the source of domestic chaos. When domestic chaos exists, it is due to selfish ambition and being deceived by Satan. James 4:2 says that sinful desires do not bring what we truly desire. Within the marriage unit, there should be a desire for peace. There should be a desire for love to coexist. There should be a desire for Jesus to be Lord over this marriage. Selfish ambition causes fighting and wars. When wars exist, there is always collateral damage. Such collateral damage may include adultery, children who war against their parents, and eventual divorce. When we allow Jesus to reign and rule the house and marriage, wars will cease, and godly bliss will become apparent. John 16:33 is a promise of Jesus overcoming the world and providing His peace. *"I have told you these things so that in me you may have peace. In the world you have trouble and suffering but take courage—I have conquered the world."*

Do not be a friend of the world which is Satan's domain. There are two kingdoms: God's and Satan's. When selfish ambition is present, Satan's kingdom is given credibility and floor space. When we allow the Holy Spirit to lead our marriages, selfishness leaves. God's peace is available and active in a God-centered marriage.

ARE TRIALS AN INDICATION THAT GOD IS PUNISHING US?

Trials and their outcomes do not refer to God punishing His people. Trials and punishment do not refer to the same process in the life of a child of God. James 1:2 tells us that when trials come our way, it is beneficial for us. Trials are challenges that are placed before us. Trials cause us to rely on the wisdom and strength of God. These challenges are everyday occurrences that may be due to sin in the world, the fallen state of mankind, or the careless actions of people. When trials come our way, they challenge our faith and produce patience within us. God allows trials and tough times to occur in our lives because He desires for us to grow closer to Him. We draw closer to God when trials exist.

Punishment is God correcting His children due to perpetual sin in their lives. There is an imposition of a penalty placed upon the person who has committed sin. Punitive measures are dealt to those who disobey the Holy God. It is important for the counselor to encourage the counselee to know the difference between trials and punishment. Proverbs 3:11–12 says that God will correct those whom He loves. God challenges the sinful choices we make and works to correct the sin in our lives. Hebrews 12:3–11 speaks to correction which is directed to a sinful child of God. Through prayer, discernment, and questioning, it will be evident if the counselee is in a period of trial or in a period where God is correcting their behavior because of their sin.

While punishment may appear to be a harsh word, it is important to differentiate it from discipline. Romans 8:1 tells us that we are not condemned by God. This is true because we are in Christ Jesus. Yet there are times when our actions are corrected by God to the extent where consequences in our lives occur. While Jesus removes all condemnation from us and eternal punishment has been removed, it appears that at times we receive correction. We seldom sin without impunity.

Galatians 6:6–7 reminds us that we are to be obedient to the Word of God. When we are not obedient and we sin against the ordinances of God, we should expect a just God to correct us. If the counselee is in a trial situation, 1 Corinthians 10:13 says that God will give them the strength to endure the trial. If, however, the person is in a sinful state, they should expect a correction to be handed down from God.

First John 5:3 tells us that if we love God, we will keep His commandments. His commandments are not burdensome to those who obey them. If the counselee is truly following God and is in Christ, there is no condemnation according to Romans 8:1. Second Timothy 3:16 says that God's Word will correct when it needs to correct.

Why does the counselee believe they are being punished by God? Is sin present? Is the sin present obvious and evident? First John 4:18 is a verse that could be used to screen this debate. Perfect love casts out all fear. Is the counselee fearful of the punishment of God? If God is truly love and we abide in God, the fear of being punished must not exist in the life of a disciple of Jesus Christ. Fear involves punishment and torment. If we are only in a state of being tried, then any counselee should not believe they are in a position of being punished. Although prophetic in nature, 2 Peter 2:9 says that God knows how to deliver people who are in trials versus those who are being punished.

As children of God, we are called to live holy lives. Ephesians 5:5–7 emphatically tells us that there is a difference between being His child and being a son of disobedience. If we are truly a child of God, sin no longer reigns and rules in our lives. If sin no longer rules our lives, there must be a change in the life of the counselee who knows Christ. Ephesians 5:8 further says to walk as children of light.

Ephesians 5:5–7 encourages us to avoid sin and walk as children of God. With the leading of the Holy Spirit, the counselee will see if trials are punishment or they are merely trials.

COMMON PSYCHOTHERAPY LABELS

The American Psychiatric Association (AMA) has developed the *Diagnostic and Statistical Manual of Mental Disorders*. This manual is purported to be an authoritative dissertation, respecting mental disorders. AMA is now on its fifth version of this manual (*DSM-V* 2013). It is from the *DSM-V* that many of the below responses are derived.

Note: Although the American Association of Christian Counselors provides resources, such as *The Popular Encyclopedia of Christian Counseling*, the sufficiency of the Bible will be evident in the below responses. Secular psychotherapy does not belong within biblically based counseling scenarios.

- a. *Bipolar*—According to *DSM-V*, bipolar disorder is defined as an individual having a manic episode or reaction to a personal situation, which may be followed by a severe episode of depression (AMA 2013).[13] Manic may be defined as hysterical, frenzied, or frantic behavior. Depression is often

---

[13] American Psychiatric Association, *Diagnostic and Statistical Manual of Mental Disorders*, Fifth Edition (Arlington, VA, 2013), Table 12.

understood as despair or hopelessness in the mind of the patient. Bipolar may be viewed as a person possessing and acting out, two potential extreme approaches to the situational analysis of life issues.

Biblical perspective—Galatians 5:22–23 tells us that there must be fruit evident in the life of a disciple of Jesus. People who are manic will display an overabundance of elation when dealing with a life situation. Galatians 5:23 tells us to be gentle and to exhibit self-control. Titus 2:12 teaches us to live stable lives. As for the depression side of bipolar, Jesus has promised in John 10:10 to give us a victorious Christian life. Depressive thoughts keep us from being victorious. Because depression affects how we think, 2 Timothy 3:16–17 should be engaged. Scripture is corrective in nature and able to guide the most troubled mind.

b. *Codependent*—This is not recognized by AMA or the *DSM-V* as being a mental disorder. According to Psychologytoday.com, codependence is defined as "two dysfunctional personalities becoming worse together" (Esposito, 2016).[14] There is a belief that the healthy partner in the relationship enables the addictive partner to continue in their addictive conduct by nurturing the unhealthy behavior. The healthy partner builds their self-esteem by caring for the ills of the unhealthy partner. Codependency may exist due to a perceived need. For example,

---

[14] https://www.psychologytoday.com/ca/blog/anxiety-zen/201609/6-signs-codependent-relationship.

wives may display codependency in their marriage because they *need* their husbands' financial support.

Biblical perspective—Galatians 5:1 speaks to the liberty we have in Jesus Christ. We are not to become entangled with the things of this world. Things here include codependency. This *disorder* is of the world. We also are told in Colossians 1:28 to teach every man to present himself perfect in Jesus Christ. Codependency allows people to stay in their condition of sin. Second Timothy 2:7 says that God has given us a sound mind, not a spirit of fear. Therefore, the fear of tomorrow, which exists in a codependent relationship, should not exist. Perpetual sin conditions must not be in the life of a disciple of Jesus Christ.

c. *OCD/obsessive-compulsive disorder*—According to the *DSM-V*, a person with OCD possesses recurrent and persistent thoughts which are intrusive and disturbing to the individual. The individual, in turn, uses an obsessive compulsion as a way to alleviate or even distract their mind from these persistent or disturbing thoughts (AMA 2013).[15]

Biblical perspective—Second Corinthians 10:5 tells us to take every thought captive to the obedience of Christ. We are able to accomplish this through the teachings of the Holy Spirit. John 14:26 says that the Holy Spirit will teach us all things. Our minds control our thoughts and thereby control our actions. Matthew 7:11 speaks

---

[15] American Psychiatric Association. *Diagnostic and Statistical Manual of Mental Disorders*, Fifth Edition (Arlington, VA, 2013), 300.3.

to a good God giving us what we need to survive in life. We should think about the goodness of God the Creator. Therefore, persistent thoughts of fear and the unknown should not possess our minds. Philippians 4:4–8 gives us a list of things we are to think about. These things provide pure thoughts for our lives.

d. *Anxiety*—According to the *DSM-V*, anxiety is viewed as excessive worry and fear (AMA 2013).[16] The worry is often characterized by restlessness, unease, and fear of the outcome of certain situations. Excessive uneasiness and apprehension are often manifested in a person burdened by anxiety.

Biblical perspective—Philippians 4:6 commands us to not be anxious about anything. Prayer and supplication to God will bring His peace to us. Matthew 6:25–34 further instructs us to not worry about our lives or worry about tomorrow. God is in charge, and He will provide. Philippians 4:19 is the promise that God will supply all our needs according to His riches in Christ Jesus. First Thessalonians 5:16–18 instructs us to concentrate on giving thanks. When we give thanks to God for his provision, we do not have the time to be anxious.

e. *Addiction*—According to the Addiction Counselor's Desk Reference, there are several models and definitions of addiction. The term *addiction* is from Latin and means "to adore or surrender oneself

---

[16] American Psychiatric Association, *Diagnostic and Statistical Manual of Mental Disorders*, Fifth Edition (Arlington, VA, 2013), Table 3.15.

to a master" (Coombs and Howatt 2005, 35).[17] Coombs and Howatt write that the moral model of addiction declares that individuals are free-will thinkers and choose their own volition, to use a mind-altering substance. When tolerance to the substance is built up in the individual and more of the substance is required to achieve a "high," addiction and dependence on the substance may ensue.

Biblical perspective—First Corinthians 10:12–13 cautions us to take heed lest we succumb to sin. In other words, we need to know that God will not place temptation in front of us that we are not able to endure. First John 2:16 says that addictions (lusts) come from the world. As regenerated believers, we are no longer of the world (2 Corinthians 5:17). Galatians 5: 16 is the encouragement to walk in the spirit and not fulfill the lusts of the flesh. Addictions are lustful. They are a surrender to things of this world. Romans 12:1–2 commands us to present our bodies to God as a living sacrifice. When addiction consumes us, we are not able to fulfill this command.

---

[17] R. H. Coombs and W. A. Howatt, *The Addiction Counselor's Desk Reference* (2005), 35.

VERBALLY ABUSIVE BEHAVIOR (HUSBAND TO WIFE) IN A MARRIAGE

Ephesians 5:25 instructs husbands to love their wives. When verbal abuse takes place, this command from God is not being observed. Love does not ooze out of a man who is in a state of verbal abuse. Ephesians 5:28 says that he who loves his wife loves himself. As we study Galatians 5:22–23, we observe the fruits of the spirit. If we act in a malicious way or have outbursts of wrath, we will not inherit the kingdom of God. When husbands are verbally abusive toward their wives, true love for their wives and the fruit of the spirit are not available.

Ephesians 4:29 is a very good verse to speak into the life of a verbally abusive husband. He is not to allow any corruption to proceed from his mouth. It does not specify the context of this command. Therefore, at all times, we are not to allow any unwholesome words to leave our mouths. We are directed to build up each other. Verses 31 and 32 of Ephesians 4 direct us to not be bitter, not to possess wrath, and not to quarrel. Instead, we are to be kind to each other. When a husband is verbally abusive to his wife, he is not following these commands of God.

When husbands are verbally abusive to their wives, there are spiritual and emotional consequences within the marriage. Psalm 9:1 shows how David praised God with his whole heart. He promised to tell all people about God's marvelous works. When men verbally abuse their wives, not only are they failing to declare the works of God, but they are also causing their wives to stumble in this regard. Romans 14:13 instructs us to not cause a brother or sister in Christ to stumble. Our Christian spouses are a brother or sister in Christ. As well when children witness marital chaos, in the home, they may be subject to sinning as a result of the fallout of verbal abuse. First Corinthian 8:9 speaks to all, including husbands, about the need to not be a stumbling block to the weak. When children are at home, we are to teach them spiritual health. They are weak and are entrusted to us to teach them (Proverbs 22:6).

Philippians 4:8–9 is a final portion of Scripture to consider. Verbal abuse does not line up with the litany of good things listed. We are to meditate on good things; we are to meditate on the things of God. When we do this, the God of peace will be with us. As it turns out, we are striving to have peace in all areas of our lives. This includes peace within the covenant of marriage. Abusive language is far outside the picture of a healthy, God-centered, peaceful marriage.

DYNAMICS OF FORGIVENESS

Forgiveness commences with repentance. First John 1:8 says that if we believe there is not any sin in our lives, then we are deceived. The following verse, 1 John 1:9, commands us to confess our sins. When confession occurs, God's righteousness is known to us. Forgiveness is the acceptance of this confession and the godly desire for us to place the sin and situation behind us. Forgiveness assists us in maintaining godly relationships. Ephesians 5:1 is the instruction to be an imitator of God. God forgives us over and over. We need to forgive as God forgives. We imitate God when we forgive.

Matthew 6:9–15 is the pattern for biblically based forgiveness. Within the Lord's prayer, we see confession, repentance, and forgiveness. Verse 14 says that when we forgive men their trespasses, God our Father will also forgive us. If we do not forgive, God will not forgive us. Everything we do, we do in the community. We accept the faults in others, knowing that we also possess faults. The dynamic of forgiveness includes our acceptance of wrongdoings.

In the New Testament, we see the Greek word *aphiemi* translated into the English word *forgive*. The original Greek word means to let go, to allow something to fall away. For us as Christians, the dynamic of forgiveness means that we allow the wrong to fall away. While the wrong placed against us may have placed us into a certain amount of jeopardy, we are to let go of the matter. Colossians 3:13 tells us to forgive one another. As we forgive, due to Christ's forgiveness of our wrongs, we bear one another's burdens.

Ephesians 4:31–32 speaks to the need for us to be tender toward mankind. When we are tenderhearted, we forgive as Christ forgave. We are being dynamic in our approach to forgiveness. Dynamic has the connotation of change taking place. When we speak to the area of dynamics of forgiveness, we realize that change occurs for us and change occurs for those who have wronged us.

We forgive because of our love for one another. First Corinthians 13:4–6 says that love endures all things. This includes wrongs against us. Love also thinks well of others. So even when someone places a fault in our lives, we are to love, forgive, and allow reconciliation to take place.

WORKAHOLIC PERSONALITY

When we speak about work and people being workaholics, often our thoughts go to Ecclesiastes 1:3. In a rhetorical sense, the author of Ecclesiastes is claiming that work and the workaholic personality are distractions from things of God. Mark 8 and Psalm 127 would agree with this perception.

People must never be identified by "what they do for a living." Workaholics have a compulsion to work. These individuals feel fulfilled when they accomplish tasks that give them self-esteem and personal satisfaction. Galatians 2:20, however, directs us to the knowledge that our lives were crucified with Christ. Therefore, we live for Christ, and we live to Christ. Mark 8:27–38 starts with Jesus directing us to consider who He is as God. When we focus on Jesus, we realize that all we need for purpose and satisfaction is found in Him.

Jesus came to suffer and die for us. His sacrifice on the cross makes us complete in who we are as His disciples. There is not any amount of labor or hard work, which will give us identity as a child of God. All we need for life is found in Jesus. In fact, verse 34 of Mark 8 instructs us to take up our cross and follow Jesus. Verse 35 says that in order for us to find our lives, we must lose our lives. The workaholic personality is attempting to accomplish everything except the loss of personal identity. Workaholism, therefore, is sin. It is against the ordinance of God.

Mark 8 continues to challenge our thoughts about work. If we gain things of the world through our work, what have we gained in terms of the spiritual well-being of our souls? There is nothing anyone can gain from a workaholic mentality that will replace the things of God. Working hard will not allow you to gain eternal life. Psalm 127 further states that all things in life must be built by God. If God is not involved in our lives, our labor is useless and in vain. Verses 4–5 of Psalm 127 claim that we will be happy when we allow God to lead our lives. God provides food, He provides children, and He sustains us. When we know that God is involved in all aspects of our lives, the need to be fulfilled through workaholism will fall away.

HOPE FOR THE ANXIOUS

Anxiety is based on fear—fear of the future, fear of relationships, and fear of the unknown. In 2 Timothy 1:7, it clearly states that God has not given us a spirit of fear. When we recognize His power and love, we recognize that God has given us a sound mind. It is this sound mind which allows us to eliminate the anxiety in our lives. God gives us this promise.

As we consider Philippians 4:4–9, we see a godly pattern of hope given to us as his children. Our joy is to be centered on God and not how we feel. Uneasiness should never exist in the life of any Christian because of the joy of the Lord being our strength.

The fruit of the spirit will exist in our lives as we allow the Holy Spirit to remove the anxiety which may exist. As we seek God through prayer and the use of scripture, we realize that His peace will drive out all our anxious thoughts and beliefs. The pattern of hope supplied in Philippians 4 may be used by the Christian community to encourage those who struggle with anxiety.

Rejoice in the Lord always—Nothing that comes against us should ever suppress our joy. Philippians 3:1 is the command to rejoice in God. When we see the word *always*, we are being instructed that in all circumstances of life, we should find the joy of the Lord. First Thessalonians 5:16 says we are to rejoice evermore, always and forever.

Let your gentleness be known to all men—When we view this phrase, we are reminded to be meek even while being provoked. We must be slow to anger and ready to forgive at all times. James 1:19 says to be swift to hear, slow to speak, and slow to anger. Our gentleness must be evident to all. They will see Jesus in us.

Be anxious for nothing—Matthew 6:25–34 commands us to not worry about anything. We are not to worry about tomorrow, for today has its own trials. Second Corinthians 10:5 says that when we take our thoughts captive, we will be yielding to Jesus Christ as our Lord. When we move away from anxiety, we will know God's peace.

Pray and let your requests be made known to God—Regardless of our circumstances, we are to let our requests be made known unto God. We are to pray and not deviate from this responsibility. First Thessalonians 5:17 is the command to pray without ceasing. Paul encourages us to know that when we pray, God hears us and will answer our petitions.

Meditate on God's Word—Verse 8 lists a total of six things by which we are to meditate. *True* things are spiritual truths we are taught and encouraged to follow. *Noble* refers to respectful, reverent, and dignified. *Just* means to be made righteous. *Pure* means without sin or error. *Lovely* means wonderful truths from God. *Good report* means excellence in the pursuit of the things of God.

Things which we have learned, we are to follow (Obedience)—Here, we are instructed to keep practicing the things taught to us. As we are taught the precepts of God, we are to follow and obey them. For the counselee, it is important for us to emphasize that when we follow God's Word, we are less likely to fall back into our sinful ways. Obedience and devotion to God assist us as disciples of Jesus.

TRANSFERRING OUR FAITH
TO OUR CHILDREN

Ephesians 6:4 gives a challenge to parents. We are told to not torment a child but rather to train a child. As parents, we are never to discipline from a position of impatience or a position of quick, ill-thought-out responses. Impatience is the catalyst for striking back before we discern any situation. Godly patience allows us to use each moment with our child as an opportunity to teach proper attitudes and godly approaches to life. We will, however, discipline when required. When discipline occurs, our emotions must be controlled by the leading of the Holy Spirit.

With the assistance of the Holy Spirit, we train and correct our children, knowing that the Heavenly Father loves them. We teach our children the principles of God from the word of God. As we teach children about God, transference of godly principles takes place. We see here the premise and belief that God is the one true God. We teach our children that God alone is the sole object of our devotion. John 4:24 tells us to worship God in spirit and in truth. While there is one God, for those of us who are Christians, we recognize the existence of the Trinity as stated in 1 Corinthians 8:4–6. We are made to worship the God who created us.

When we are commanded to love God, there is a clear expectation that all of our love and devotion is focused on Him only. In John 14:15, Jesus says that if we truly love Him, we will keep His commandments. We must love God with all our being. Matthew 22:36–40 echoes this. We love the Lord our God with all our hearts, souls, and minds. We love God because He first loved us (1 John 4:19). When we do this, we are able to love our neighbor as ourselves. By fulfilling this command, we follow the teachings of God. As we fulfill this command, through obedience, we transfer this principle to our children.

The words spoken here in Deuteronomy 6:4–9 are to be on our minds at all times. As we practice this, we will teach these principles to our children. Psalm 119:11 says that as we hide God's Word in our hearts, we will not sin against Him. As we teach, we model. As we model, we transfer knowledge. This is why the instructions here in Deuteronomy are so important. Any time we breathe, we keep the precepts of God at the tips of our tongues. When we feel discouraged, we do not allow corruption to flow from our mouths (Ephesians 4:29–32).

In Hebrew, the word *teach* infers the need for repetition to occur. In order for us to transfer knowledge to our children, regarding the things of God, we repeat the goodness of God. When we are at home or away from home, we teach our children. We teach the covenant of God, which is the reconciliation through the shed blood of Jesus at all times. Reviewing, teaching, and obeying the teachings and commands of God must be second nature to us. In other words, the Holy Spirit will teach us all things according to John 14:26. As the Holy Spirit teaches through us, we transfer the goodness of God onto our children.

MARITAL INTIMACY

As we consider 1 Corinthians 6, we see Paul talking about all sexually immoral sins. These sins include not only sex outside of the covenant of marriage but also sexual gratification. We are to flee pornography, movies, books, and the like. The marriage covenant is the only place where sex and the thought of sex should be occurring.

First Corinthians 6:19 reminds us that we are a temple of God. As temples of God, we are to flee every lustful desire. Galatians 5:16 gives us encouragement. As we walk in the spirit, we will not fulfill the lusts of the flesh. Romans 12:1–2 claims for us to present our bodies to God as a living sacrifice. When we engage in immoral sexual sins, we are not fulfilling God's call on our lives to stay pure.

However, as we consider 1 Corinthians 7:1–5, we see that men were discouraged from having sexual intercourse with women. The context was regarding the city of Corinth and how sexual corruption had overtaken the lifestyle. The reference here is dealing with sexual immorality outside of the godly union of marriage. Paul declares that sexual immorality is not taking place when a man has sexual intercourse with his own wife. In fact, God's plan for marriage is that sex consummates the relationship. Husbands and wives are to be one flesh.

First Corinthians 7:3 commands husbands to provide their wives godly affection. Every Christian wife is to have affection placed upon her by her Christian husband. There is not anything sexually immoral suggested against a husband who shows affection and promotes sexual intimacy within the covenant of the Christian marriage. Sex is not the husband's prerogative nor the wife's duty. According to this portion of Scripture, there is a mutual agreement regarding the act of sex.

Sexual deprivation here refers to the act of sex and also the withholding of romance within the covenant of marriage. Christian husbands and wives are not to deprive each other as the temptation to sin outside the covenant of marriage will be great. There is a provision here to abstain from sex for a short duration of time in order to fast and pray.

God has ordained the covenant of marriage. When we counsel, we instruct on the knowledge that a godly, Christ-centered marriage is attainable. While it is attainable, the godly marriage is the plan of God for Christians. Sex within marriage is appropriate. Sexual immorality of any sort is not permissible within a Christian marriage.

REGRET OVER PAST SIN

There are not any *redos* in life. We are not able to take back our sinful actions or the pain that sin has caused. However, as we read these verses, we are encouraged to know that God can *reset* our lives. As counselors, we must encourage counselees to understand that as they are led by the Holy Spirit, spiritual healing is available to them. It is possible for the shame from past sins to fall away.

When we walk in the light of God's Word, we have the ability to be purified. As we say that, we know that sinless perfection is not possible. When regret from past sin pervades our lives, we are not walking in the light. Indeed, when we do not fulfill this commandment, we are sinning. There is a need for the biblically based counselor to remind counselees that confession is needed for past sins. When confession is made, we allow the blood of Jesus Christ to wash over the sins. First John 1:7 is the promise of Jesus cleansing us from *all* sin. There is a departure from the sin and a letting go of the sin once confession has been made. Remorse for past sin should not linger when we know that Jesus died to cleanse us. We emphasize the need for the counselee to receive forgiveness. When forgiveness is received and acknowledged, the sin of regret falls aside. We must realize and know that the shed blood of Jesus is enough to wash away a multitude of sin.

First John 1:8 addresses those who are in a state of sin. If people are lingering in sin, then obviously, repentance and confession have not occurred. Anyone in this condition does not have any right to claim they are free from sin. But if you have confessed your sins, as stated in 1 John 1:9, then God will cleanse you. It is in the cleansing where the regret for past sin must be washed away. We are not allowed to have regret for any past sin once we have taken it to Jesus.

Romans 3:23 says that we continually sin and fall short. As Jesus is noted as the advocate for us (1 John 2:1), He intercedes for us. Due to the fact that we have the perfect advocate who will deal with our sin, we must hold to the promise that we have been forgiven. Jesus is the propitiation for us. According to 1 John 2:2, Jesus is the only one who has stood between an unholy man and a Holy God.

Regret from past sin says that we do not truly believe that Jesus is the intermediary for us. There is an unspoken belief that Jesus is not enough when we have regret from past sins. We must confess this wrong thinking and know that Jesus died to take away our sins.

AUTHORITY AND SUFFICIENCY OF SCRIPTURE (BIBLIOLOGY)

Bible's Claim to Authority

We might commence this discussion with the consideration of Deuteronomy 4:2. The word of God carries with it power and authority. As a result, we see here in Deuteronomy that we are not to add or subtract from its pages. The authority is complete; we are to accept the commands as given to us in the scriptures. Jesus reiterates this in Matthew 5:18, "Until heaven and earth pass away, the authority of God's words and grammar within the Bible will not pass away." The word of God and its authority will stand forever.

Jeremiah is told by God to write down everything told to him because it is the authority of God by which Jeremiah prophesied (Jeremiah 30:2).

Moses called the word of God the law of God, and the witness from God against man (Deuteronomy 31:25–26).

In the high priestly prayer of John 17, Jesus says to the Father that all God has given to the son, He (Jesus) has passed on this authority to the disciples. Furthermore, the apostle Paul in 1 Corinthians 14: 37 makes the bold claim that what he has written are the commands of God.

Psalm 119:160 tells us that the entirety of God's word is truth. God's judgments and His authority live forever.

In the following question on inspiration, we will view 2 Timothy 3:16–17; these verses talk about the authority of God's word to correct and instruct. These instructions equip a Christian for every good work.

Finally, Matthew 4:4 shows us that the word of God will sustain men and women. It is the authority of God by which we live our lives.

GOD THE FATHER (THEOLOGY PROPER)

Godhead

In Christianity, God the Father is often considered the first person of the Trinity. In Colossians 1:3, God is recognized as the Father of Jesus Christ. When we call the Father the first person of the Trinity, we must ensure that we do not marginalize the Son and the Holy Spirit. Each person within the Trinity has a unique and distinctive role.

However one wishes to view the Trinity—hierarchical versus egalitarian—the Father coexists and is coeternal with the Son and the Holy Spirit. We must also state that by calling God the Father, the first person of the Trinity, we do not imply that the Father created the Son.

God the Father sent the Son to redeem mankind. The Father's ministry is initially exclusive as He gave an assignment to the Son, Jesus Christ. There was not any other entity in all the universe who had the power to give this assignment. John 16:32–33 speaks to the Father being with the Son. There was ministry within the Godhead at the time of the crucifixion. Today, there is mutual, continual support for ministry within the Trinity.

We see in Galatians 4:4–5 the ability for everyone to be adopted through the shed blood of Jesus. The Father testifies to the Son and the work the Son accomplished on the cross. John 5:19 emphasizes that the Son cannot do anything apart from the Father. When Jesus ascended to the right hand of the Father, the Holy Spirit was then sent to dwell among men. The sending of the Holy Spirit was involved in the Father's plan to redeem mankind.

God also is a perfect and true Father. Part of the ministry of God the Father is to show His love toward us. Romans 5:8 tells us that while we were still separated from God the Father, He sent the Son to save us. The scripture 1 John 4:8 further instructs the reader that God is love. Because God is love and He is the perfect Father, we are to love like He loves. Along with supplying love to fallen man, God ministers grace and peace to us (Philippians 1:2; 2 Thessalonians 1:2).

Lastly, we recognize the ministry of the Father through the lens of John 3:16. God loved us and continues to love us so much that Jesus was sent to die. There is a redemptive ministry from the Father toward mankind noted in this verse. There is also this sense of perfect planning from the Father. Due to His wonderful plan of redemption, we have the ability to be reunited with the Father because of the shed blood (Hebrews 9:22).

WHAT THE FATHERHOOD OF GOD DOES IN OUR LIVES

For many of us, there is a tainted view of Fatherhood. We must be able to view God as the perfect Father. It is only through the leading of the Holy Spirit and the reading of God's word that this might be realized.

We ought to view the Father through the lens of biblical history. When we consider God's plan for man and His redemptive plan for man after the fall, this writer is fascinated by how loving God is to His creation. Only a true Father would be this engaged in our lives.

We are created in the image of God (Genesis 1:27). Even after the fall of man in Genesis 3, God lovingly looked after His people. We benefit directly from the fact that the Father has sustained us throughout history. Only a true and valid Father would be this concerned about His creation. Although we are not perfect people, God loves us as individual people who need to be reconciled to Him.

Psalm 68:5 speaks to God being a Father to the Fatherless. This is a comfort as God looks after His creation. He is the perfect Father, giving us comfort, support, and love. Psalm 139:13 claims that the Father formed our inward parts. When we know that God the Father created us to be His children, we take solace in the knowledge of His care for us.

We love God the Father as a perfect Father. For that matter, we also must love the Trinity. But when we talk about the Fatherhood of God, we receive a view of healthy parenting. God parents us with respect and love and disciplines those He loves (Proverbs 3:11–12; Hebrews 12:5–11). In Luke 15, we see the forgiveness of the Father when we mess up (prodigal son). In the life of this writer, proper parenting and nurturing from the Father is absolutely everything.

There is reassurance for all, with the knowledge that God is in heaven (Matthew 6:9). When we consider who God is as our Father and realize that He shines down upon us, we are blessed. We know that God's kingdom is forever. Psalm 145:13 says that the Father's kingdom is forever. Lamentations 5:19 makes a further claim about the everlasting kingdom of God. For this writer, there is an expectation that God the Father will look after me.

For this writer, there is an expectation that I will be loved, forgiven, and restored by the Father. For this writer, there is an expectation that God will lead me and guide me into all truth. When God is viewed as the perfect Father, all fear is gone. In Isaiah 43:1, "Do not fear…you are mine."

ATTRIBUTES OF GOD

God is an immense God. In fact, His character, His qualities, and His abilities are incomprehensible to the finite minds of humans. It is always an important discussion for us to consider the attributes of this great God. For the sake of this book, the author has contributed and discussed five attributes of God. It is hoped that the reader will take the time for further exploration when it comes to God and His attributes.

Goodness of God

God is good, and everything about God is good. God is the ultimate and final standard of goodness. When we speak to His definition of goodness, we must state that the commandments of God are the benchmark for morality and ethics. We survive in a community due to the statutes of a good God. The Ten Commandments in Exodus 20 are the commencement of this standard. In Exodus 34:6, "He abounds in goodness and truth." John 8 tells us that the truth of God and His Son Jesus will set us free. God is good to supply us with His truth. James 1:17 speaks to God supplying us with every good gift.

Holiness of God

God is holy. Isaiah 6:3 declares the holiness of God. *Holiness* is defined as God being separated from sin. Due to sin in the world, Jesus needed to be the propitiation for us (1 John 4:10). Jesus is the link between a Holy God and an unholy human race. When we accept the sacrifice of Jesus on the cross, we are consecrated, set aside, and given His sanctifying gift. The Holy God is not connected to sin. There is not any part of the Holy God being corrupted. This lack of corruption speaks to His goodness.

Immutability of God

God does not change. In fact, it is *impossible* for God to change. James 1:17 says that there is no variation in God nor shadow of turning. In Revelation 1:8, God claims that He is the beginning and the end. Therefore, He cannot change. Lamentations 3:22 offers us the promise that God's mercies never end. In Malachi 3:6, "I am the Lord; I do not change." For the Christian community, this attribute is important. God has established promises to us which will remain forever.

Eternal God

Eternal has the connotation of always being in existence. The Trinitarian God has existed forever. Revelation 1:8 reminds us that God is the beginning and the end. For one to make this claim, there needs to be an understanding that He does not possess a beginning or an end. John 5 and 1 John 5 promise the believer that they will possess everlasting life. This is only possible when God, who is eternal, fulfills this promise in those who are reconciled to Him. God is outside of time. Yet for our understanding, we believe that eternity will be in place after we gain heaven. (*Note*: Many scholars would say that eternity begins the moment we are genuinely saved—cf. John 17:3; 1 John 5:11–13.)

God is love

According to 1 John 4:7–8, love is of God, and everyone who knows God will love like God. John 3:16 says that God loved the world so much that He sent His Son to die. John 15:13 is about love being so great that Jesus died for His friends. There is this deep affection that God has for us. We are His creation, and therefore, He has our best interests at heart. Love is an emotion. Love is also an action as we see in the word agape in 1 Corinthians 13. God supplies this emotion to us to live in society. Passion for God comes from His desire for us.

DECREES OF GOD

God's decrees are His pronouncements and declarations for humanity. It is God and God alone who has the authority to make these decrees. Romans 8:28 tells us that God works out all things for our good. This is a decree from a loving God. He ordains the paths of a righteous man. Ephesians 1:3 gives us the decree of promise that all spiritual gifts are from a Holy God.

God's decrees speak to His character; in Exodus 3:14, "I am Who I am." God's decrees speak to sanctions of morality; in Exodus 20:13–14, "You shall not murder, You shall not commit adultery." God's decrees speak blessing; in Matthew 3:17, "This is my beloved Son."

Ephesians 2:10 says that we are His workmanship; God has ordained this. He has authorized us to be His workmanship. We walk in the decrees of God. His commandments and laws for us are perfect. Psalm 139:16 tells us that God has decreed and proclaimed the number of days we are to live.

There is this sense of kingdom when you consider God's proclamations for us. Only a righteous king would decree good for His people. God is the author and finisher of our faith. He is the authority and proclaimer of our faith. God does not seek wise counsel from others before He declares a proclamation for His people. Hebrews 12:2 reminds us that Jesus was sent by the Father to put faith in place. Jesus came to establish faith in our lives.

Hebrews 11:6 is a further complement to our discussion. Because of the decrees of God and the establishment of faith in our lives by Jesus, as we possess faith, we will please the one true God. He has made this decree to and for us.

God has decreed a future for us. He has decreed an eternal purpose for those who trust and put their faith in Him as Father. John 5 speaks to us gaining eternal life through Jesus. God has proclaimed that He will reign and rule forever (Psalm 146:10). Romans 11:33–36 gives purpose and majesty to the decrees and affirmations of God; His judgments and ways are perfect.

GOD THE SON (CHRISTOLOGY)

We identify with Peter that Jesus is the Christ the Son of the living God (Matthew 16:16). The term *Christ* will be interpreted to say anointed one. Jesus was anointed and appointed by God the Father to enter into the world of fallen man in order to redeem man (1 John 4:9). John 1:14 tells us that the word (Jesus as God, Jesus as man) came to dwell among mankind.

Colossians 1:15 says that He is God incarnate and the firstborn. Colossians 1:16 says that Jesus is the creator; He was present with the Father and the Holy Spirit when creation occurred. In John 1:2, "He was in the beginning." Because of Christ's love for creation, He went to the cross to redeem us from a potentially lost eternity. Eternal life is the gift we receive from the Father through the Son (Romans 6:23). Jesus is life; He has come to give us life and allows us to live abundantly (John 10:10).

Along with this thought, we know that Jesus is the Son of God (John 1:34). God tells us that He is His Son, and He is well pleased with Him (Matthew 3:17). He is also the lamb of God and Messiah who will take away the sins of the world (John 1:29). *Messiah* is defined as Jesus being the deliverer of man from an eternity destined for hell. While Jesus is the Son of God, we know that He is fully God. Jesus is Deity. The scripture 1 John 5:20 states that Jesus is the true God, and He is eternal life. (This will be explored more in the discussion of Jesus's deity.)

Jesus is the Savior of the world. He was the final sacrifice (Hebrews 10:10–14). He came to seek and save those who are lost (Luke 19:9–10). According to John 3:16–21, all who accept Christ's sacrifice on the cross will be saved, and those who reject Jesus as Savior will be condemned. Along with being our Savior, Jesus is to be our Lord. Lord is defined as being the head of a household. For Jesus to be Lord of our lives, He must be the leader of our lives. Romans 14:8–9 asserts that Jesus is our Lord. Because He came to be our Lord, He died to reconcile us to God our creator.

Jesus is our propitiation; He is the link between sinful man and a Holy God. Jesus fulfilled the demands of a Holy God for reconciliation to exist with a sinful man (1 John 4:10). Romans 3:24–25 speaks to the fact that Jesus's shed blood deals with the sin nature of man. Colossians 1:20 notifies us that there is peace through the shed blood on the cross. Ephesians 1:7 confirms redemption in the shed blood of Jesus Christ. So Jesus is my Lord, He is my Savior, and He is my brother (Hebrews 2:11).

DEITY OF JESUS

Deity means that Jesus is God. As we study the word of God, we see an abundant amount of evidence to prove that Jesus is God. Jesus is Deity. In Isaiah 9:6, His (Jesus) name will be called wonderful counselor, the mighty God. The Old Testament spoke of Jesus (Messiah) coming to earth as the one true God. Micah 5:2 says that Jesus will come to earth as God; He is from everlasting. Due to the monotheistic nature of Judaism and Christianity, any false claim to being God was considered blasphemy. Matthew 27:43 is where Jesus claims to be the Son of God.

God had previously declared this in Matthew 3:17, "My Son in whom I am well pleased." Titus 2:13 makes the bold claim that Jesus is our great God and Savior. The life of Jesus on earth demonstrated that He was Deity. Jesus then had two distinct natures while He walked on earth. He was all God while being all man (Colossians 2:9–10). In Him, the fullness of the Godhead dwells. While He walked the earth as a man, He led a sinless life (Hebrews 4:15). Only God, someone who claims to be divine, could accomplish this feat.

John 1:1 claims that the word (Jesus) was God. Jesus, as God, actually makes this claim regarding His person; "I and the Father are one" (John 10:30). This mirrors the claim in

Matthew 27 about being the Son of God. Jesus is worshipped as God. In Acts 7:59, Stephen calls upon Jesus as his God to receive his spirit. In the high priestly prayer of John 17, in verse 5, Jesus asks for the Father to glorify Him before the world existed. Jesus is claiming that as God, He existed before the worlds were created.

Due to His nature as God, Jesus performed miracles. John 2 is the miracle of turning water into wine. There is this action, this miracle performed by Jesus which adds to His claim of Deity. Luke 5:1–11 demonstrates that Jesus had divine authority to perform miracles. Although the disciples had fished all night, Jesus as God told them to let down their nets as they would reap a great harvest. Jesus predicted this miracle as He was truly God.

In John 10:30, Jesus claims that He and the Father are one. This is the claim that they both are God. John 8:58 Jesus makes the bold claim that before Abraham existed, "I am." This is parallel to the claim of God, "I am who I am" (Exodus 3:14). In 1 Corinthians 15: 57, we see that God, as Jesus, broke the power of death. We as Christians have the victory over death because of the shed blood of Jesus Christ. God came to live among us and give us the ability to live the victorious Christian life.

HUMANITY OF JESUS CHRIST

Jesus did not attend earth to experience man's pain and suffering. As God, He already understood the lostness and agony experienced by mankind due to the fall in Genesis 3. Jesus's relationship with man in the Garden of Eden was before His incarnation. Although He had not yet walked on the earth, He knew the hopeless condition of all humans. As we note in Hebrews 2:10, Jesus then came as embodied man in order to "bring many sons to glory."

John 1:1 declares the deity of Jesus Christ. He was fully God. Philippians 2:5–11 speaks to Jesus humbling Himself, coming to earth as a man and going to the cross as a human to shed His blood for the sins of the world. Although Jesus was God, He took on the form of a bondservant and died for you and me. Jesus, in human form, demonstrated love and humility.

Hebrews 1:3-4 speaks to Jesus coming to earth to purge our sins. After the crucifixion, Jesus then ascended back to His home in heaven. Colossians 2:9 declares that in Jesus, God was made manifest in the form of a human being. He came to seek and save those who were lost (Luke 19:9–10). He came as a man; He continues to come to us as God.

CHRISTIANITY AND THE LAW OF SEPARATION

Jesus took on the form of an earthly human so as to demonstrate His love for us. Romans 5:8 tells us that while we were yet sinners, Christ died for us. This shows us love in action. But as Jesus ministered on earth, His love for men and women was evident. As we read about the woman at the well in John 4, we see Jesus's compassion for her lostness. We see Jesus reaching out to her, in human form, and teaching what it means to worship God in spirit and truth. Jesus also showed His love and care for the adulterous woman in John 8. Here, we see Jesus challenging the accusers of this sinful woman. His charge to them, whoever has never sinned, throw the first stone. Jesus needed to attend to earth in human form for man to be reached at his lowest point.

When Jesus speaks to the woman in John 8, He enquires her about the location of her accusers. At the point of this question, her accusers have left. Jesus then lovingly says that she is no longer condemned. However, in a human counseling setting, Jesus tells her to go and sin no more (John 8:11). As a sinless human being (Hebrews 4:15), Jesus ministered to those who were lost without Him. In this verse, we see the ability of all to stand up to temptation demonstrated. True, only perfection would never sin, but we do have a high priest who showed us how to flee from sin and temptation.

Finally, we know that Jesus came as the second Adam. Romans 5:15 says that through the sin of a human, many people perished. However, through another man, Jesus, grace from God the Father came to mankind. Romans 5:18 reminds us that through one man's righteous act, justification came to all who will believe. Where sin abounded, grace through the life of the man Jesus abounded much more (Romans 5:20).

GOD THE HOLY SPIRIT (PNEUMATOLOGY)

When Jesus came to earth, He promised us that we would not be alone. John 14:26 aids us in this thought; the Holy Spirit will teach us all things. It is the leading of the Holy Spirit by which biblical counselors minister. There are three distinct ministries of the Holy Spirit in terms of interacting with mankind. Due to space and time, these three will only be marginally explored. There are the with, in, and upon experiences noted as we read the Word of God.

The Holy Spirit is *with* men convicting them of their sins (John 16:8). There is the *indwelling* of the Holy Spirit (John 20:22; receive the Holy Spirit). There is the *upon* experience of the Holy Spirit. (Acts 1:8; receive power when the Holy Spirit comes upon you).

With respect to the Holy Spirit being God, we see evidence of this in Genesis 1:2. The Spirit of God, Holy Spirit, hovered over the earth. Psalm 143:10 speaks to the Spirit of God being good. Isaiah 11:1–5 speaks to the sevenfold ministry of the Holy Spirit. Psalm 51:1 is a plea for the Spirit of God to not leave King David. This is evidentiary to the knowledge of the Holy Spirit being Deity. The verse 1

Corinthians 2:12 tells us that we have received the Spirit of God, Deity, that we may know the things of God.

In Acts 5:1–5, Ananias and Sapphira lied to the Holy Spirit. There is the claim that they have not lied to man but to God. Acts 28:25–27 is a quote from Isaiah 6, claiming the Holy Spirit, Deity, spoke through Isaiah the prophet. Finally, Hebrews 10:15 declares that the Holy Spirit (God's Spirit) witnesses to us.

The personhood of the Holy Spirit, His unique individuality, is also evident throughout the scriptures. Romans 8:9 is the key to understanding who we are in Christ. If the Holy Spirit is in us, we are of Christ. If the Holy Spirit does not indwell us, we are of the world. If the spirit of Christ, who raised Jesus from the dead, dwells in us (Romans 8:11), our mortal bodies receive life.

Romans 8 goes on to state that the Holy Spirit intercedes on our behalf. Verse 17 of this chapter is a reminder that God's Spirit witnesses to our spirit that we are His children. Ephesians 4:30 speaks to the role of the Holy Spirit to seal us. The scripture 1 Corinthians 2:10–14 talks about the ministry of the Spirit of God. It teaches and reveals the truth to man and aids us in judging all things. The Spirit of God has the role of being a comforter, teacher, and guide to those who trust in Jesus as Lord and Savior. As biblically based counselors, we *must* be led by the Holy Spirit of the one true God.

THE TRINITY

There is only one true God who eternally exists in three persons: Father, Son, and Holy Spirit. When we use the word *Trinity*, there is an immediate sense of unity within the Godhead. Ecclesiastes 4 talks about the strength of a three-cord strand. This is modeled within the Trinity. Although there is an indication of God the Father being the head of the Trinity (2 Corinthians 1:3; 1 John 3:1), all three persons in the Trinity are coequal and coexistent. We must realize that the three persons of the trinity have distinct roles.

Matthew 3:16–17 mentions all three persons of the Trinity. This is evidentiary knowledge of the existence of the Trinity. The Trinity is not some contrived, designed concept of man or theologians. There is unity realized in this portion of scripture. Within the Godhead is the understanding that each role supports the other two roles. Matthew 12:28 is further evidence of the Trinity. As mentioned above, all three persons of the Trinity are noted. Matthew 28:19 commands us to make disciples and ensure that the Trinity is given credit for discipleship.

We see in Genesis 1:1 that God the Father created all things. The Holy Spirit is noted to be present during creation (Genesis 1:2). Colossians 1:15–17 is proof that the Son of

CHRISTIANITY AND THE LAW OF SEPARATION

God, Jesus, was also present at the moment the world was created. These verses give credence that all three roles within the Trinity support one another. God the Father also has the distinction of sending the Son to die on the cross and redeem mankind (John 3:16). God the Father has appointed the Son to be the judge of the world (John 5: 22; 27). God the Father loves the Son and shows Him all things (John 5:20).

Jesus, the Son of God, is the savior of the world. In 1 John 2:1, it claims that Jesus is the advocate to the Father. It is through His shed blood that we receive salvation. John 3:16–20 tells us that belief in Jesus will give us eternal life. If you reject Jesus's plan for you, then you have condemned yourself to eternity in hell. John 19:28 shows that Jesus knew all things were accomplished through His crucifixion. John 19:30 is His claim that the work on the cross was now finished.

Jesus also came to live among men. Jesus was fully God while being fully man. Philippians 2:5–11 explains how Jesus gave up His rights and descended to earth for the express purpose of redeeming sinful man. When He was on earth, He was the example to us on how to live a victorious, abundant, Christian life (John 10:10). Hebrews 4:15 claims that Jesus did live on earth and while on earth lived a sinless life. The scripture 1 Thessalonians 4:16–17 is proof of Jesus returning to earth and setting up His kingdom.

John 14:26 has been cited several times in this text. It is, however, necessary to remind us that the Holy Spirit is the comforter, teacher, and guide for mankind. The Holy Spirit, as a part of the Trinity, will teach all things to men. Romans 8 speaks to the role of the Holy Spirit interceding on our behalf. Galatians 5:22–23 lists the fruit of the Spirit. It is this spirit that allows us to possess emotional intelligence.

That is to say, we hold our tongue, think logically, and live in a community because of the Holy Spirit. Although men have written about keeping our emotions in check, it is only through the leading of the Holy Spirit that this occurs. Self-control must be evident in our lives.

    Trinity is in existence. It is by the Trinity that we are able to live out our Christian lives.

THE MINISTRY OF THE HOLY SPIRIT IN THE CONTEXT OF COUNSELING

The greatest advantage to the biblically based counselor is the presence of the Holy Spirit. Jesus commands us in John 14:15–17 to keep His commandments. Furthermore, He promises that another helper, the Holy Spirit, will come to be with us forever. When we counsel, we counsel with truth. John 14:26 tells us that the Holy Spirit is available to minister truth to the lost. The advantage then is the knowledge of the Holy Spirit leading and guiding our thoughts and words in the counseling process. He will give us the words to say to the counselee (Romans 8:26–27).

The Holy Spirit is available to convict people of their sins (John 16:8–15). This truth must never be overlooked. The Holy Spirit will teach truth. The Holy Spirit glorifies Jesus and points people to the gift of salvation through the Son. When we become regenerated, the Holy Spirit witnesses to our spirit that we are children of God (Romans 8:16).

The Holy Spirit will declare these things to mankind. Romans 8:9 says that if the Spirit of God dwells in us, we will not abide in the flesh. The Spirit of God gives us life.

Galatians 5:16 aids us in the counseling process; walk in the Spirit and you will not fulfill the lusts of the flesh.

The Holy Spirit gives life to all who will accept Jesus as Savior. Ephesians 5:18–19 reminds us to be filled with the spirit. Filling by the Spirit only takes place when we are redeemed and is an ongoing repeated yielding of our lives to Him. Ephesians 1:13–14 is the promise of being sealed by the Spirit who guarantees our inheritance.

With the spirit indwelling us, we are able to worship the one true God. The spirit of God allows us to worship in spirit and in truth (John 4:23–24). When we have the spirit of God imparting wisdom to us, the fruit of the spirit is evident (Galatians 5:22–23). Fruit needs to be present when we counsel those who are hurting or are engaged in sin.

When we sit with counselees, we are sitting in a discipleship relationship. We instruct these people about Jesus. We then lead them into a discussion about Christian living. In order for any Christian to follow Jesus, the Holy Spirit must be the lead counselor. Titus 3:5 is the guarantee that we will be renewed by the working of the Holy Spirit. We are but servants of the Most-High God. Therefore, when we counsel, we counsel with humility, knowing that the Holy Spirit is ministering to lost souls and those who need to come back to the cross.

DESCRIBE THE MINISTRY OF THE HOLY SPIRIT IN RELATION TO THE WILL OF GOD

The will of God dictates for all regenerated people to live an abundant Christian life (John 10:10). For this to occur, the will of God must be manifested to the church (universal) and those who abide in the church. Matthew 28:19–20 and Mark 16:15–16 give the will of God; "go and make disciples." Sanctification occurs within the human heart when we place our lives into Jesus, and we then pursue the abundant life which God intended for us. Galatians 5:22–25 encourages us to live abundantly in the spirit and walk in the Spirit.

Discipleship is the will of God. The scripture 1 Timothy 2:4 demonstrates that God wishes all people to come to Him to be saved and to know the truth. John 14:1–6 is one proof text stating that Jesus has gone away to prepare an eternal place for those who are regenerated—those who are His disciples. Matthew 25:31–46 is the opposite of this promise. This portion of scripture is a warning to all who are not regenerated, for they will go away into everlasting punishment. John 14:26 shows us how the Holy Spirit will teach and show us all things. This teaching includes the understanding of the will of God.

John 16:12–33 shows us how the Holy Spirit is engaged in this sharing of truth. The Holy Spirit will share the truth of God the Father. That is to say, the Holy Spirit will guide us into the will of God. The Holy Spirit is the lead counselor when it comes to discipleship and abiding with one another within the universal church. As people accept Jesus as Lord and Savior and enter the church, the Holy Spirit will declare the words and ministry of Jesus (John 16:14–15). "To be filled with the Spirit (regeneration) means to be caught into the joy that flows among the Holy Trinity."[18] This is the core of discipleship and ultimately core to the will of God.

As part of the will of God, there is the knowledge that the Holy Spirit transforms people. In Greek, the word *paraclete* is found in John 16. This word is translated as helper, advocate, and encourager. When we consider this word, there is additional evidence that the Holy Spirit is involved in seeing that the will of God is fulfilled in people and in the church. The Holy Spirit is all about transformation. The verse 1 Corinthians 3:16 instructs us to know that the Holy Spirit has transformed us. We are now a temple of God. Acts 7:48–50 and Acts 17:24 say that God does not dwell in a temple made with human hands. The ministry of the Holy Spirit is involved in the will of God by transforming lives through His indwelling presence.

Isaiah 11:1–2 speaks about the ministry of the Spirit of God upon Jesus, Messiah. It is this working of the Holy Spirit which puts into motion the will of God. The Spirit will rest upon Him and give wisdom, understanding, counsel, might, knowledge, and the fear of the Lord.

---

[18] John Piper, Retrieved 2020-09-24, https://www.desiringgod.org/messages/be-filled-with-the-spirit.

MINISTRY OF THE HOLY SPIRIT IN RELATION TO GOD'S WORD

As a biblical counseling consortium, we agree and affirm that the scriptures are sufficient for any counseling process. It is through the illumination of the Holy Spirit that the truth of God's word is revealed to mankind. John 14:26 is an important verse as it constantly reminds us that the Holy Spirit is given to us to teach us all things. Teaching of all things includes the revealing of truth from the word of God.

Second Peter 1:3–4 is a parallel verse to John 14:26. In this, we take note that God has given us all things which lead us to life and godliness. These are the things spoken about earlier. The Holy Spirit enlightens us on the things of God, *all* things of God. Furthermore, we note in 2 Timothy 3:16 that all scripture is given by inspiration from God. It is the working of the Holy Spirit in the lives of men where this inspiration takes place. Divine authorship of the scriptures comes from the Holy Spirit. Furthermore, the Holy Spirit gives us sound advice as to how to apply scripture in a counseling setting.

The natural man, he who is without God, cannot understand the things of God or the word of God (1 Corinthians

2:14). This verse tells us that only the Spirit of God can reveal the things of God. Prior to this verse, we see in 1 Corinthians 2:9–11 where the spirit of God reveals the things of God. This includes revelation from the word of God and how it is applied to our lives. According to 1 John 2:27, wisdom and leading from the Holy Spirit are all necessary for us to minister the word to counselees. The meaning of text and context of scripture come from the Holy Spirit. We abide in Christ and are led by the Holy Spirit who in truth will not mislead us. The meaning within the word of God is revealed to us through the Holy Spirit, the perfect counselor.

Psalm 119:11 promises us that as we memorize and meditate on God's word, we will not sin against Him. The Holy Spirit is the person who ministers this to us. When we follow God's word, we have the ability to walk in the spirit. When we walk in the spirit, we will not fulfill the lusts of the flesh (Galatians 5:16). Jesus is the word (John 1:1). The Spirit testifies to the word, and therefore, the Holy Spirit applies God's word. The Holy Spirit guides us into all truth and assists us in applying His Word (John 16:12–14).

MAN (ANTHROPOLOGY)

Man's Nature

Man's natural tendency is to be separated and to desire separation from his creator. Man was created in the image of God and yet chose to rebel against the creator (Genesis 3:1–7). Due to the corruption which ensued the fall of man, in his natural state, man cannot appease a Holy God. Natural (sinful) man does not understand the things of God (1 Corinthians 2:14). There is not any spiritual discernment within the heart of a person who has not been regenerated or restored to a right relationship with his creator. Therefore, man's nature is a complete separation from his God and creator. Man lives in darkness. Matthew 6:23 tells us that the darkness in man is great; it is contrary to the hope given to us through Jesus Christ.

Separation is a horrible thing. When friends and family die, we grieve due to the separation. There is a parallel here to our lives with God. Due to being separated from the Holy God, death brings grief into our lives. Separation causes death. It is only through the shed blood of Jesus that regeneration and reconciliation can occur (John 3:16–21).

Everlasting life is available to fallen man. We are no longer separated from the creator.

When we describe "human nature," we are describing the inner core of people. In a worldly setting, fundamental belief in feelings, psychology, and the way people think form a piece of this understanding. Human nature in itself is sinful. There is absolutely nothing anyone can do to connect with a Holy God. It is important to reiterate that secular psychotherapy does not belong in biblical counseling. If man is by nature evil and sinful, how can anything from the mind of man be healthy for the counseling process?

We (man) are so ungodly. Jesus had to come to earth to be the propitiation between a Holy God and an unholy man (1 John 4:10). There had to be this link in the relationship. Men love darkness rather than light because their deeds are evil (John 3:19). Current condition of every man's nature is to embrace evil intent. Jesus is the light of the world. Light shines in the darkness and exposes the sin nature within each human being (John 8:12).

MAN'S CURRENT CONDITION

Man is separated from God. If man's nature is depicted as being sinful, then his condition is depicted as being lost in his sinful state. The spiritual condition of man is further defined as being corrupt. Corruption cannot inherit the kingdom of God. When we speak of being lost, we recognize death is present. Sin has caused man to be separated from a Holy God. This separation means that we are living on the cusp of eternal death. Romans 5:12 speaks specifically about death being present in unregenerate man.

We know from Romans 6:23 that the wages of sin or the sinful condition is death. Ephesians 2:1 gives us hope that while we were dead to sins, we are able to be alive in Christ. As mentioned above, Romans 5:12 says that death has come to all people due to the sinful condition of their hearts.

With sin being the enemy of our soul, we comprehend that the only solution to escaping eternal death is through the shed blood of Jesus. Hebrews 9:22 makes the claim that without the shedding of blood, there is not any remission. The scripture 1 John 1:8 reminds us that if we believe we do not have a sinful nature, we are being deceived. There must be a recognition of this condition. It is through this recognition that regeneration may take place.

Due to the sinful, lost condition of man, there is, according to Galatians 5:17, a war being waged between flesh and spirit. The apostle Paul further claimed in Romans 7:18 that there was nothing good in him. Paul recognized the need for regeneration to occur in his life and be therefore reconciled to his creator. Genesis 3 is the record of the fall of man. Romans 7 is a testament to the fallen, sinful, corrupt condition, causing us to fight this spiritual battle.

The condition of lost man may be further defined as alienation or separation from the God who created us. Philippians 2:15 gives evidence to the understanding that mankind, this generation, is corrupt. Ephesians 4:22–23 speaks to the old, sinful, lost man growing corrupt through deceitful lusts. Romans 6:11 makes the claim that we were dead to sin. Corruption exists as the condition of man.

DEPRAVITY OF MAN

Due to the fall of man, as noted in Genesis 3, all people are born with a sin nature. Without the assistance of the Holy Spirit, it is impossible for anyone created by the Holy God to avoid being engaged in sin. Depravity of man indicates that man is fallen and corrupt in nature because of original sin within the Garden of Eden. For the sake of this paper, this writer will not speak to the Calvinist versus Arminian depiction of total depravity.

On our own, it is impossible for us to avoid sin and follow the commandments of a Holy God. Jeremiah 17:9 tells us that the heart of man is deceitful above all things and desperately wicked. Ephesians 2:1–3 says that we are dead in our trespasses and sins. By nature, and due to the fall, we are children of wrath. Depravity means to be wicked and morally corrupt. It is important for the biblically based counselor to present this belief to the counselee. Without Jesus's shed blood and the indwelling Holy Spirit, no one can alter their depraved, corrupt state. The indwelling of the Holy Spirit must be present in all people in order for the depravity of their souls to be purified.

We present the definition of depravity to the counselee. John 3:19 expressly states that men love darkness rather than light because their deeds are evil. Corruption is the natural inclination, and by default, people will move toward it as they navigate their lives. The verse 1 Corinthians 2:14 tells us that the natural (depraved) man does not understand the things of the Holy God. We pray and hope that the response to this presentation is the acceptance by the counselee that they are a sinful, corrupt person. Secular psychotherapy does not bring this corrupt state into the conversation.

Inherently, psychotherapy and science believe people are good and righteous. There is this premise that humans' interactions with other humans are improving. Sam Harris claims in his book, *The Moral Landscape*, that this is so; "Despite our perennial bad behavior, our moral progress seems to me unmistakable."[19] As Christ-followers we assert that it is only through the acknowledgment of Jesus as Lord and Savior that man's inherent, sinful nature may be restored.

Because of the sinful, depraved nature of man, there is this chasm between God and His creation. We have need of a savior. Ephesians 2:8–9 explains to all that it is only through the finished work of Jesus on the cross that depravity in man can be eliminated. Yes, we continue to war after the flesh. However, we do have sanctification placed within us by the shed blood of Jesus. We present to the counselee that if they genuinely wish to be free from their depraved state, they must accept Jesus Christ as Lord and Savior. In John 8:36, "If the Son has freed you, you are indeed free from your depraved life."

---

[19] Sam Harris, *The Moral Landscape: How Science Can Determine Human Values* (New York: Free Press, 2010).

PRESENT-DAY SELF-ESTEEM THEOLOGY

Secular psychotherapy places credence and authority on the theory of Maslow's hierarchy. Within this hierarchy is the striving to obtain self-actualization. Self-esteem has at the core of its definition, the desire for people to become self-fulfilled and self-actualized while understanding their self-worth. As we consider the theology of self-esteem, we quickly recognize the self-seeking nature of this quest. Psychotherapy does not belong in biblical counseling because of the focus on the improvement of mankind without the involvement of God the creator.

There is a void in the heart of every human being. Often, this void is not understood nor is it defined. People ask: "What is my purpose in life? What is my self-worth? What is my significance?" As Christians, our only purpose is to worship the one true God. The void then is the separation between our nature and the nature of God.

It is due to the purpose of loving and worshipping God that the chasing of the theology of self-esteem is nullified. When we pursue after the heart of God, our selfish desires drop off. Luke 4:8 states clearly that we are to worship God and only serve Him. The chasing of self-esteem causes us to serve ourselves. Remember, Holy God does not yield to an unholy man.

Self-esteem speaks to the selfishness of people. There is a striving toward self-confidence, self-respect, and being a self-made person. When these statements become the focus of our lives, we move away from the dependency on God. The high standard of self-esteem dictates the pursuit of self-care. Self-care is the belief that if a person looks after their well-being and mental health, they will be able to assist others who are struggling with issues of life. When we stand back from this belief, we should see that it is only the work of the Holy Spirit that heals the heart of sinful man.

We are created in the image of God. Due to this fact, there should not be a discussion regarding the theology of self-esteem. Genesis 3:7 shows us that being created in the image of God was not enough for Adam and Eve. They were told that they could be like God. Their eyes were dull toward the deceit and delusion of self-esteem. They were chasing their desires instead of the desires of the one true God. Self-deception is an aspect of self-esteem in that it moves people toward an emphasis on self and not God the creator. Colossians 2:8 is a warning to not follow false teachings and therefore be self-deceived.

Within the theology of self-esteem comes the acknowledgment of self-help. Self-help calls for the reliance on our own strength and resources. In his book, *Your Best Life Now*, Joel Osteen makes the claim, "All of us are born for earthly greatness…you were born to win."[20] There is this belief that if you work hard and believe in yourself, you will achieve greatness. Osteen contends that striving after greatness is our life goal. We know that this is not the will of God the Father for His creation, His children.

---

[20] Joel Osteen, *Your Best Life Now* (New York: Faithwords, 2004).

CHRISTIANITY AND THE LAW OF SEPARATION

When we are truly regenerated people, our goal is to acknowledge our need for the Father and the shed blood of Jesus Christ. We do not strive for earthly greatness. Psalm 139:5–6 is a reminder of the protection we receive from the Father. We strive to worship the one true God who gives us this protection. Reliance on God and not self-reliance is truly the desired pursuit of all disciples.

BELIEVER'S NEW IDENTITY IN CHRIST

The scripture Second Corinthians 5:17 is one of the proof texts for being new creations in Jesus Christ. When we accept Jesus as savior, our old life dies, and our life then becomes new. We recognize that all things are from God. God the Father has reconciled us to Him through the shed blood of Jesus Christ. Our identity is no longer viewed in corruption but is viewed through justification. Galatians 2:16 says we are vindicated by Jesus Christ.

Romans 6:4–11 speaks to our position in Christ. Once we accept Jesus, we walk in the newness of life. This is not the rebirth of physical life but of spiritual life. We are no longer slaves to sin but free from sin. The end of verse 11 tells us that we are alive in Christ. Ephesians 1:13–14 shows how the Holy Spirit brings newness into the repentant believer and then seals them for redemption.

Galatians 2:20 speaks of Christ physically being crucified. The apostle Paul moves this into a spiritual sense. Christ's crucifixion is regarded as though we were actually crucified with Christ. Once we accept Jesus, we have this new identity. We are moved from the category of a sinner and into the category of a saint. We now live, not in our own strength, but Christ's life in us brings about this newness.

Jesus's supreme sacrifice is our only escape from the law, sin, and power they have over our spiritual lives.

First Corinthians 15:46–58 gives a further glimpse into the realization that we have a new identity in Jesus. Through Adam (Romans 5:18–21), sin entered the world, and through sin came death. Jesus as the second Adam came to reverse this corruption. When we are considered heavenly beings (regenerated), we are changed. While our physical bodies are corrupted due to sin, our new identity in Christ allows our spiritual beings to be incorruptible. When we put on this incorruption (1 Corinthians 15:54–55), we are new creations within the atoning work of Jesus on the cross.

Galatians 5:16 further speaks to our position in Christ. If we walk in the spirit because of salvation, we will not fulfill the lusts of the flesh. When we do not fulfill the lusts of the flesh, the fruit of the spirit, as noted in Galatians 5:22–23, exists within our new identities. Verse 24 of Galatians 5 says that we who are Christ's put on the new identity of being crucified to the flesh.

SALVATION (SOTERIOLOGY)

Defining the Term, Being Saved

Regeneration is the key component to understanding salvation or being *saved*. Regeneration involves the admittance of perpetual sin within humanity and the need for humanity to acknowledge this sin. It is sin that initially caused the separation between man and a Holy Creator God. Regeneration is defined as receiving new life due to the shed blood of Jesus Christ. Man must accept the work of Jesus on the cross as the solution to perpetual sin (Ephesians 2:8–10). This acceptance is the action required to convert a sinner into a saint. When this conversion occurs in the life of a person, being saved is the outcome.

But what are we being saved from, and what are we being saved to? When we talk about being saved, there is this sense of safety, of being rescued, and the removal of persons from harm. In Genesis 1:1, we see in the beginning God created all things. As we read the creation story, we see everything was good. Yet in spite of excellence, Adam and Eve were deceived in the garden and decided to be gods on their own level. When sin entered the world, as described in

Romans 5:18–21, all of mankind entered into a position of depravity. This depravity is defined as corruption as acts of evil. Depravity also states that death was brought into the picture. With the sin nature being inherent in all mankind, we are all doomed to spiritual death unless we accept Christ's ability to save us from this death.

Because of sin entering creation, all of humanity is separated from a holy, sinless God. With separation in mind, we understand that not one person can experience eternal life on their own merit (Ephesians 2:8–10). God in His wisdom sent Jesus to die on the cross for us. It is through the death of Jesus on the cross and the shedding of His blood that salvation or being saved from our sins can be realized. We are, therefore, saved from the sting of sin and the sting of death (1 Corinthians 15:42–58). John 3:17 makes the bold claim that we are not liable to the punishment of death if we accept the saving, redeeming message of Jesus Christ and repent of our sins. We are being delivered and saved from eternal death. Jesus is the Holy One who allows us to be reconciled to the Father. His finished work on the cross saves us from damnation.

WHY IT IS ETHICAL TO TALK ABOUT THE GOSPEL IN A COUNSELING SESSION

We are commanded by Jesus to go and make disciples (Matthew 28:19; Mark 16:15; Luke 24:47–48). When we have the opportunity to speak the truth of discipleship into the lives of counselees, we tell the gospel message. It is due to the shed blood of Jesus that the counselee may find true freedom (John 8:36). The truth of the gospel brings healing, comfort, and compassion into the lives of these counselees.

As a biblically based counselor, it would be remiss and irresponsible of us to not talk about Jesus. Only Jesus brings *genuine, long-lasting* healing. Only Jesus allows us to live the victorious Christian life (John 10:10). Only Jesus gives us power for service and ministry due to the indwelling Holy Spirit (Acts 1:8). When the counselee sits with us, we must assume that this may be the only opportunity to connect with this person. When we understand the sense of urgency in any counseling setting, we will present Jesus. Yes, there is a sovereign God who through the leading of the Holy Spirit nudges people into counseling (John 16:8). But we also know that

Satan is at work (1 Peter 5:8). Satan will attempt to thwart any meeting we may have with individuals.

It is the opinion of this writer that not presenting Jesus would be unethical. How could we withhold information regarding the greatest opportunity for people to be free from the condemnation brought about through sin? John 12:26 commands us to follow Jesus, and through the following process, we will serve Him. Service to Jesus means we are constantly in the process of presenting Jesus to the lost. We must also remember that while any counselee may have stated that they have received Jesus as Lord and Savior, we present the gospel to ensure that regeneration has actually taken place. As well, the good news of Jesus continues to disciple all who have received a regenerated spirit. In Christ, all shall be made alive (1 Corinthians 15:22).

Psychotherapy within a Christian counseling setting may actually interfere with the introduction of Jesus. The American Christian Association for Psychological Studies demands its members to hold adequate education in their respective field in order for psychotherapy to be present in the counseling context.[21] While this may be their respective standard for operations, it must be reiterated that Jesus is the only solution to a fallen world.

When we consider our call to be disciples of Jesus Christ, we must move away from the ethical demands of a secular society. If we genuinely believe that Jesus is the way, the truth, and the life (John 14:6), we must ethically present this to all counselees. For any counselor to withhold this information would be unethical.

---

[21] https://www.caps.net/membership/.

IMPORTANCE OF BRINGING A COUNSELEE TO CHRIST

Isaiah 14:12–17 speaks to the fall of Lucifer—Satan. Due to arrogance and pride, Lucifer decided that he would not worship the one true God. Since his fall, he has set out to deceive all people. Through the fall of man, Lucifer was able, through evil intent, to introduce sin into the world. The verse *2 Corinthians 11:14* speaks to Satan being an angel of light, and his deception continues. Satan's influence on people causes them to sin. This sin nature shows how people are separated from God their creator. It is, therefore, of extreme importance to lead people to Christ—the anointed one.

We always want to take ground back from the satanic forces in the world. *Ephesians 6:12* says that we wrestle against spiritual wicked forces. (There will be further development of this in the demonology section.) This is why at every opportunity we tell people of the hope of the gospel. If we know that Jesus saves us from eternal damnation, we must warn those who do not know Him.

We spoke earlier about making disciples of Jesus Christ. *Matthew 28 and Mark 16* are the texts which bring us to this conclusion. We are commanded to go and make disciples.

This includes discipleship in the context of counseling. *Luke 24:46–48* fleshes this out more for us. It was necessary for the anointed one to die for us. We pass this truth on to the counselee. Repentance and the remission of sin take place when this truth is accepted by anyone who hears. All nations, which includes people groups and individuals, must have this told to them. *Matthew 24:14* instructs us to preach the gospel to all nations before the end comes. All of these notes are commandments for us to follow as counselors.

God created all mankind to worship Him. *Isaiah 43:21* speaks to God creating Israel, His people, to worship Him. *John 4:23* speaks to the woman at the well; she was told to worship God in spirit and in truth. *Psalm 95:6* asks us to kneel down and worship God. All of this to say true worship of God our creator cannot occur unless a person is regenerated. Therefore, it is highly important that we tell counselees about Jesus, so they may live a victorious Christian life and worship the one true God.

THE ROLE OF BAPTISM

Ephesians 2:8–9 instructs us to know that we come to Christ by faith and faith alone. *Verse 9* specifically states that there are not any works done by man, which will provide salvation. Baptism is the outward sign that an inward change has taken place. We, therefore, view baptism as a religious ceremony that in no way affects one's ability to know salvation through Jesus Christ. (*Note*: For the sake of this discussion, this writer will only refer to *water* baptism and not the "baptism of the Holy Spirit." The question above does not differentiate between the two.)

There are Christian groups that do believe that water baptism is tied to salvation. *Acts 2:38* is one proof text for this held belief. It states that people should be baptized *for* the remission of sins. In reality, this verse should be translated *due to* the remission of sins. Baptismal regeneration is contrary to the word of God. We believe that it is only through God's sole act of grace whereby anyone can be truly saved. In fact, the writer of this report, while being the president of a Christian college, dismissed a professor due to his relentless teaching of water baptism being mandatory for salvation.

Galatians 2:16 reminds all of us that works will never factor into the saving message of Jesus Christ. Faith in Jesus is the only hope of the world. Justification comes from Jesus, not a religious ceremony. *Titus 3:5* makes a further claim to this; His mercy keeps from us the penalty of death which we deserve. Jesus saved us through regeneration and the indwelling of the Holy Spirit.

Romans 3:24 also says that redemption, the forgiveness of sins, is God's act of grace through Jesus Christ. *Romans 6:23* claims that the gift of God, eternal life, is available through Jesus Christ. *Philippians 3:9* is a great verse for this discussion. It says that nothing of my own, including water baptism, can produce faith or justification. It is only faith in Christ, the righteousness of God, by which we are saved. Salvation is by divine grace only, and no works of man's righteousness can appease a Holy God.

We read in *1 Corinthians 15:1–4* where Paul gives the summary of saving grace and salvation. He does not make any mention of the need for water baptism within this synopsis. Christ died for our sins; nothing more is required.

GREATER INTIMACY WITH GOD

When we speak to the term *intimacy*, we refer to increasing our knowledge of people and their respective personalities. This knowledge is not surface knowledge but has at its core the belief of deep familiarity and understanding of someone. Greater intimacy with God may then be defined as our need and desire to know Him more, know His commandments more, and commune with Him more in spirit and in truth. *John 4:22* is the command to worship who we know. *Philippians 2:12–13* says we are to work out our salvation with fear and trembling. It is said that while our salvation is by the grace of God and not by any righteous act of man, we are compelled to place a maximum effort into our Christian walk.

Hebrews 11:6 starts this discussion for us. This scripture clearly instructs us to pursue after God. Faith is the catalyst to our pursuing the Holy God. Faith comes by hearing. The more time we spend with God, the more of His words we will hear and obey. We come to God because we believe who He is; He is holy and desires for us to become holier. The scripture *1 Peter 1:15–16* instructs us to become holier. He who calls us to this standard is Himself holy. Greater intimacy with God is accomplished by reading His word, meditating on His word, and having dedicated time in His presence. Greater intimacy with God is ongoing sanctification.

John 8:32 tells us that the truth will set us free. The initial truth of this speaks to sanctification being received upon our belief in Jesus as Lord and Savior. We are set free from the burden of sin; we are set free to worship the one true God, and we are set free to counsel people with the hope of the gospel of Jesus. *Romans 6:14* promises us that sin will no longer have dominion over us once we receive salvation and sanctification through Christ. *Verses 16–17 of Romans 6* claim that we are now slaves of righteousness. Ongoing sanctification, this greater intimacy with God transforms who we are in Christ. The scripture *2 Corinthians 3:18* instructs us to know this truth because of the leading of the Holy Spirit.

Hebrews 4:14–16 tells us that we can obtain grace and mercy in times of need. As we draw closer to the heart of God, by spending time in His presence, we become more Christlike. When we need strength, we rely on God to work in our lives through the leading of the Holy Spirit. We attain greater intimacy, not via our own strength but by asking God to implant new intimacy into our lives. *First John 4:4* tells us that greater is He that is in us than he that is in the world. The truth of this promise says to us that we can attain greater intimacy if we desire greater intimacy. Holy Spirit will fulfill this promise.

SATAN (DEMONOLOGY)

In *Romans 7:13–25*, we witness the struggle of good versus evil that existed in the life of the apostle Paul. For all Christians, there is this tension between good and evil. We are continually at war with our flesh while desiring to serve the one true God. *Romans 6:6–7* says that we are no longer slaves to sin. In fact, we are free from the burden of sin due to the shed blood of Jesus. Spiritual warfare is the battle that rages on between good and evil. By defining spiritual warfare, we give recognition to the fact that it exists.

When we consider the spiritual world, we quickly understand that there are two kingdoms. There is the kingdom of God, and there is the kingdom of Satan. God is good, Satan is evil. Here in lies the tension. God is waging a war against Satan. Satan is fighting back. As Christians, we are involved in this battle, this piece of spiritual warfare. While we may not wage war directly against Satan, we wage a war against his minions and his children of darkness. Christian warriors are called to fight against the powers of darkness. Spiritual warfare is our involvement as warriors in the fight against Satan's evil intentions.

Ephesians 6:10–18 speaks specifically to the issue of spiritual warfare. The war is real. If evil did not exist, there would not be a war. However, in this passage in Ephesians, we are told that there is a war against spiritual wickedness against wicked leaders in high places. Yes, this is in the spiritual sense, but it is also in the physical sense. There are rulers present and in this world who hold physical positions of power and are pure evil. As a retired police officer, and someone who has a measure of discernment, this writer witnesses spiritual warfare daily. Spiritual warfare is the influence of evil on the hearts of men and the ensuing battle to thwart this influence.

Secular psychotherapy and modern medicine want people to believe that there is no such thing as the boogieman, the demonic. In fact, there are Christian denominations that state that Satan does not exist. There is either willful blind ignorance of the work of Satan, or he has completely blinded the eyes of those who are in darkness. The scripture *2 Corinthians 4:3–4* speaks about the god of this age blinding the eyes of people. Psychotherapy does not have a place in the church of Jesus Christ. Psychotherapy does not deal in a bold, godly manner with spiritual warfare.

Isaiah 14:12–17 (many Bible scholars also believe that Ezekiel 28:13–17 speaks of Satan's fall) tells the story of the fall of Lucifer. It is this fall from perfection, which leads to the fall of man. The fall of man has put in place sin. Sin causes death. For the Christian, spiritual warfare involves the belief that we need to be on guard. *First Peter 5:8* reminds us that Satan will devour people. After all, if Lucifer willfully fell from grace, he will attempt to make others fall as well. The battle is real and will be in our faces until we die or Jesus returns in triumph.

SATAN, THE GREAT DECEIVER

For the sake of this answer, Lucifer, Satan, and the devil will be synonymous terms. In Hebrew and to the children of Israel, Satan is noted as the master deceiver and adversary of God. In *Isaiah 14:12–17*, we see original perfection existing in an entity known as Lucifer. However, Lucifer decided that being submissive to God the creator was not a desirable notion. Due to free will existing in his heart, Lucifer decided to challenge God and God's leadership. Lucifer left the majesty of heaven, took other angels with him, and set up his own kingdom. Satan exists because of his rebellion against God.

Lucifer or Satan is viewed as a fallen, deceived, and evil angel. He is a spiritual creature whose master intention is to take over the world. The scripture Second *Corinthians 4:3–4* calls Satan the god of this age. He comes to blind the mind of humans. The rationale for blinding peoples' minds is so the control of their beings might occur. We know as we read this portion of scripture that the god of this age attempts to block the message of Jesus Christ from penetrating the hearts of people.

First Peter 5:8 documents how Satan moves over the earth attempting to deceive and devour. This is proof of his plan of being the master of this world and the ultimate deceiver. *John 8: 44* calls Satan a murderer from the beginning. He attempts to take to hell with him all who will listen to his deceptive message. Satan speaks against the truth, is a liar, and is the father of all lies. *John 10:10* is the further claim of Satan being a thief, a murderer, and a destroyer.

Satan, the master deceiver, has always had evil intent. In the Garden of Eden, Satan was the voice of the serpent who deceived Eve. *Genesis 3:1–5* gives the account of how Satan came to interfere with the creation of God. As stated in *John 8:44*, he is the father of all lies and the father of deception. His intent is always evil. He is the reason that spiritual warfare exists.

Satan attacks the mind and tries desperately to control the thought processes of all humans. The scripture *Second Timothy 3:13* is realized in present times while also being prophetic in nature. Evil men, who follow the master deceiver, Satan, will grow worse and worse. Our minds are blinded now and will become worse as evil grows. *Second Corinthians 10:3–5* encourages us to take every thought captive to the obedience of Christ. There is the claim within this verse that every thought is not captive. Indeed, Satan is moving forward with his intent to control the world.

As we study *Revelation 12:4–5*, we are reminded that Satan's primary purpose is the destruction of the Christ-child. Satan's purpose is in place today, and it will continue into the future. Satan is going to be defeated in the end. The Christ-child and the message of Jesus will never be thwarted by Satan. *First Thessalonians 1:10* gives us this promise. *Revelation 20:10* speaks about the devil being defeated and cast into the lake of fire. So although Satan roams around devouring people, he is already a *defeated foe*.

THE CHURCH (ECCLESIOLOGY)

Biblical counseling falls under the authority and oversight of the body of Christ—the church.

Note: For the sake of this discussion, there will be an assumption that we are referring to a God-fearing, biblically based *local* church.

We attend church to hear the preaching of the word. *Hebrews 4:12* exhorts us to know that God's word has the ability to pierce the hearts of all men. We also attend church to worship God. *John 4:23* tells us to worship God in spirit and in truth. As we look at the word of God, we believe that worship is conducted individually, and it is conducted in a corporate setting. *Colossians 1:28* commands us to teach all men. The body of Christ, the local church, is the vehicle by which we follow this commandment. Furthermore, *Colossians 2:8* warns us about worldly philosophy and the deceit of men. Therefore, we preach that Christ is crucified through a healthy, local church.

Ephesians 4:11–12 speaks to the responsibility offered by God to leaders within the church. The evidence for the existence of these positions sits in the action of equipping saints. There is a biblical authority provided to these individuals to equip the saints. Within this responsibility also lies the overview of accountability. *Acts 20* and *1 Peter 5* charge the elders of the local gatherings and churches to shepherd the flock. As shepherding occurs, the local leaders and the local church are able to give oversight to all counseling processes. Biblical authority for discipleship sits within the purview of the church. Church leaders will ensure that all counselors, within the church context, will be competent to counsel.

It must, however, be known that counseling is not merely the responsibility of the leaders listed in *Ephesians 4*. All people who have genuinely been regenerated and are bearing healthy, Christlike fruit may be engaged in counseling processes. *Proverbs 27:17* encourages us to challenge one another on our walk with God.

Matthew 28:19 and *Mark 16:15* is a call to the local church to make disciples. As disciples are made, the follow-up is the discipleship of these individuals. *Hebrews 10:25* exhorts us to gather together. It is through the gatherings that people are taught, exhorted, and edified. It is within these gatherings that people are stirred up to love and good works. These actions include counseling. The scripture *1 John 1:3* is a parallel verse that challenges us to declare the gospel of Jesus Christ. One aspect of declaring the message of Jesus is through counseling. This will be and should be completed within the context of the local church. (*Note*: We cannot deny that God also uses parachurch organizations that are committed to the Scriptures and point their mentees to the local church. IABC, The Navigators, Word of Life, and Bible colleges and seminaries are good examples when they are bibliocentric.)

The church is the body of Christ. *Acts 7:48* is the statement saying that God does not dwell in the temple made with human hands. God's Spirit dwells in the hearts of the regenerated, born-again believers. These believers have the ability to counsel under the accountable structure of the local church. Within the structure of the local church is the ability for all believers in Jesus to gain competency in the area of counseling. When God dwells within us, there is not anything we cannot do for Him as we are led by the Holy Spirit (please see Romans 15:14).

BIBLICAL COUNSELING DOES NOT FALL UNDER THE AUTHORITY OF PSYCHOLOGY

If psychology was as good as it claims to be, why is the world so messed up? Yes, Satan has put into action a rebellion against God, hence the messed-up state of humanity. However, psychological interaction outside of the actions of the one true God is a blueprint for failure. In fact, psychology in general moves people away from reconciliation with the God who created us. So while psychology may make the claim of being a healthy science, it does not offer Christ-centered hope.

Within secular psychotherapy is the opportunity for self-help—self-actualization. But as we study *Genesis 3:1–5*, we quickly realize that our attempt to live without the presence of God is a quick trip into misery. Personal self-ambition was the cause of the fall of mankind. Biblically based counseling must not be attached to or under the authority of psychology.

The Holy Spirit was promised to us as a helper. *John 14:26* makes the bold claim that the Holy Spirit will teach us all things. If this is true and we follow the one true God, then biblical counseling must be subjugated to this same God.

The scripture Second *Timothy 3:16–17* tells us that scripture brings forward the cure for the ills of the world. The word of God, not psychology, challenges, corrects, and instructs the walk of generations of men and women.

Psychology is pseudoscience. It focuses on the human mind and how the human mind operates. Biblically based counseling focuses on God, His word, His Son Jesus Christ, and the Holy Spirit. Because of this brief definition, we quickly can see that those secular beliefs and ungodly teachings in the scientific community do not mix with God and His word. We do not believe there is a contradiction with science when it is properly defined.

Psychology does not offer reconciliation with God. *Galatians 6:1* instructs us to restore a brother in Christ who has stumbled. There is hope in this. *Ephesians 4:31–32* gives us instructions on how to live our Christian life. We are to love, forgive, and experience forgiveness. Psychology and psychotherapy focus on self-care and self-reliance while often avoiding reconciliation with fellow man and God.

Psychology does not deal with the admission of wrongdoings or even entertains the notion of depravity and sin. God's word convicts, challenges, and causes mankind to live in the community. *Colossians 3:12–13* allows us to see how we should live in a community. When we share life with one another, when we pray for one another and walk life's journeys with one another, we experience the hope found in Jesus Christ. Psychology does not allow for this type of hope in a godly community. Biblical counseling falls under the authority of God that is administered through the local church.

ACTIVE CHURCH PARTICIPATION IS VITAL FOR THE COUNSELOR AND COUNSELEE

Colossians 3:16 speaks to the action of challenging and admonishing one another. If this is true of a church community, then this cannot be accomplished by individuals living in isolation. Further than this is the verse in *Romans 15:14* where the word of God states that we teach and confront one another within this church community. We affirm then that church participation is vital and mandatory for all disciples of Jesus Christ. This then is valid for counselors and counselees.

If *Ephesians 5:19–21* is true that we worship together and submit to one another, then this is only realized within the context of church. *Hebrews 10:25* commands us to not forsake the assembling together of one another. God has not hardwired the individual to live alone. In *Acts 2:40–47*, we see a true church community in operation. Unity existed, and the church grew. Apostles' doctrine was taught, and they grew in the grace of God. If someone was in need, these hard-pressed individuals were upheld by the local group. Engaging in church activity aids all of us in living the victorious Christian life (*John 10:10*).

For the counselor, church participation is a must. Because we believe in the authority of the church, the counselor submits and falls under this authority. The scripture First *Timothy 3:15* says the church is from the living God and the pillar of truth. Counselors and counselees need to participate in a God-fearing local church so as to hear the truth. In the same fashion of obedience to the counselor, counselees need to submit to the governing authority of the church which has been instituted by God.

We attend church so that we will receive support. *Galatians 6:2* says that we should bear one another's burdens. Bearing one another's burdens is extremely true within the context of counseling. While we wish to not break confidentiality, we still have the ability to pray for one another. Furthermore, the pastoral staff within each church should have the ability to assist situations that become complex and difficult to direct.

Romans 12:3 tells us to not think more highly of ourselves than reality allows and to think soberly. The local church, while flawed, will be able to assist each counselor and counselee navigate this premise. *First Corinthians 3:18* allows us to see that we may not be as wise as we believe. Church participation allows us to lean on godly wisdom from others who attend church with us.

Jesus stated in *Matthew 16:18* that He would build His church. If Jesus is the founder of the church, which we do believe to be true, then church participation assists all of us in hearing the truth of the gospel. When a believer submits to the loving leadership of their local church and biblically based spiritual leaders, believers are placing themselves under the watch care of shepherds who are charged to *"shepherd the flock of God"* (1 Peter 5:2).

CHRISTIAN LIVING (PRACTICAL THEOLOGY)

Is counseling alone sufficient for the long-term maturity of the counselee?

In terms of formal counseling appointments and settings, no. There is clearly an aspect of community life where we are being engaged in the life of the counselee. Counseling does form a piece of living in the Christian community, but it is not the completion of the community. *Acts 2:40–47* is an example of this. While the early church did exhort, admonish, and counsel, they also broke bread together. They concerned themselves with the physical and spiritual well-being of brothers and sisters in Christ. There was a holistic approach to discipleship and the church community. Clearly, this is an example of current church situations. Maturing is living a disciple's life.

Matthew 28:19 and *Mark 16:15* tell us to go and make disciples. It is the humble opinion of this writer that discipleship is more than counseling alone. *Acts 14:21* suggests that a part of discipleship is actually leading people to Christ. As we lead people to Christ, we teach, counsel, and encourage. *Hebrews 10:25* says we gather together to exhort one another.

Counseling and encouraging are activities formally used in this environment. Counseling is not the sole activity of the Christian community nor the sole maturing activity of disciples of Jesus.

Titus 2:4 instructs older women to teach younger women. This could be in a one-on-one counseling session, or it could be in a larger gathering. Maturing of saints in Christ is a lifelong endeavor. Counseling may be long term, but often, counseling is committed to short-term, specific issue matters. *Second Timothy 2:2* speaks of Paul's charge to Timothy to take his (Paul's) teaching and teach other men. When we teach others, it may or may not be in a counseling setting.

Romans 12:4–8 gives us a model of gifts. Within this model is the understanding that teaching, exhortation, and leading are involved. Through this portion of scripture, we do notice that counseling exists; however, it is not the sole gift given to the body. *Ephesians 5:19* gives us the understanding to speak to one another with various forms of worship. *Hebrews 3:13* tells us to exhort each other daily so that we could avoid wandering into sin. We live in a community, which is more than just counseling.

HOW DOES BIBLICAL COUNSELING RELATE TO THE BIBLICAL MANDATE OF DISCIPLESHIP?

Being a disciple of Jesus Christ is a lifelong activity. As has been stated previously, we have the mandate in *Matthew 28* and *Mark 16* to make disciples of Jesus Christ. In *Matthew 4:19*, Jesus says to the disciples that He will make them fishers of men. Discipleship was in the early teachings of Jesus and the early church.

We see a beautiful picture of discipleship in *Luke 9:23*. If we truly wish to follow Jesus and be His disciple, we pick up our cross and follow Him. This is where counseling comes into the picture. When people struggle with this concept, when people struggle with sin and taking up their cross, we sit with them and teach them the pattern of discipleship from the word of God. In order to follow Jesus, to be a true disciple, we deny ourselves and give Jesus permission to lead us and guide our lives (Psalm 32:8).

Disciples need to be taught these concepts. Biblically based counseling is an opportunity for these teachings to take place. We accept the rejection of the world each day and follow the one true God. Biblically based counseling speaks this truth into the life of the disciple of Jesus—the counselee.

John 14:26 gives hope that needs to be passed on through the counseling process. The Holy Spirit teaches all things to all genuine believers. As He teaches, there are times when, as counselors, we come alongside people to help them navigate the teachings. We exhort, admonish, and give correction where necessary. God the Father gives complete provision for every disciple of Jesus for every situation of life. Counselors know this, understand this, and point counselees toward biblical answers. All of this forms a piece of discipleship.

Biblical counseling is rooted in the word of God. Thoroughly grounding itself in discipleship, biblical counseling points wayward disciples back to the cross of Christ. The scripture Second *Timothy 3:16–17* reminds us that all scripture is profitable for doctrine, teaching, and correcting the disciple of Jesus Christ. *Colossians 1:28–29* is a call to teach every man, warn every man, and present him to Jesus who is the perfecter of the individual's faith. These verses prove how biblical counseling fits succinctly into the mandate of discipleship counseling.

SANCTIFICATION IS A LIFELONG PROCESS, NOT A ONE-TIME EVENT

Justification and righteousness are *imputed* upon the believer once they accept Jesus Christ as Lord and Savior. By *imputed*, we mean these works of salvation are completed through the shed blood of Jesus. *First John 4:10* speaks to Christ being our propitiation. He is the link between Holy God and unholy man. When we come to Christ, sanctification is placed upon us in that we may now approach a Holy God through the shed blood. *Hebrews 9:22* says that without the shedding of blood, there is not any remission of sins. Sanctification, however, is ongoing; it is a progressive work of Jesus.

First Peter 1:16 commands us to be holy as God is holy. This is a direct quote from *Leviticus 19:2*. These scriptures indicate that although we are children of God, there is more holiness that can be obtained for our lives. The scripture Second *Corinthians 3:18* says that we are growing and changing to be more Christlike. Becoming more Christlike means that sanctification or becoming holier is an ongoing, lifelong process.

Colossians 3:10 explains how, as disciples of Jesus Christ, we are changing into His likeness. *Philippians 2:12–13* gives direct teachings about our Christian attitude. We are to continue to pursue after the heart of God. Jesus Christ in us causes us to do everything for the glory of God. When we work out our salvation, it is the Holy Spirit in us that causes this change. It is clear in *1 Corinthians 1:30* that Jesus became our sanctification. However, initial sanctification upon salvation is a portion of complete sanctification. *First Corinthians 6:11* instructs us to know that the Holy Spirit washed us and sanctified us upon the act of our salvation. Complete sanctification will never occur until we physically die or Jesus returns for His church. It is progressing as we mature in Jesus. *Hebrews 12:2* indicates that Jesus is still working on our holiness. He will be the finisher of our faith. He has started a good work in us and will complete it according to *Philippians 1:6*.

The scripture Second *Thessalonians 2:17* indicates ongoing sanctification. Jesus is establishing us in every good word and work. *Galatians 5:16* says to walk in the spirit so that we will not fulfill the lusts of the flesh. These lusts war against the spirit of God. These lusts are contrary to the word of God. This indicates that sanctification is progressive. *Galatians 5:22–23* shows us that operating with the fruit of the spirit is an ongoing development. If the litany of sins listed before the fruit of the spirit in *Galatians 5:19–21* is directed to disciples of Jesus (which it is), then that means that sanctification is something we need to pursue. It is, however, only through the Holy Spirit that we recognize love and joy for one another.

MARRIAGE AND FAMILY
(BIBLICAL SOCIOLOGY)

Biblical roles of the husband and wife

Hypotasso is the Greek word noted in *Ephesians 5:21*. This word is translated as submitting. It means to be subjective, to obey, to submit yourself unto. There is a call for all Christians to be in the position of submitting one to another. As we commence the discussion of the specific roles of husband and wife, we initially remind ourselves that Christian brothers and sisters need to have a submissive approach to godly relationships. We die to ourselves. *Galatians 2:20* says we are crucified with Christ.

The initial submission for all believers in Christ occurs when we come to Christ and accept Him as Lord and Savior. We submit to His leadership because of His love for us and our love for Him. *Romans 5:8* says that God's love was so great that while we were still sinners, Christ died for us. Men are called to lead their households. *Ephesians 5:23* tells us that husbands lead their wives and ultimately lead the house. The scripture *1 Timothy 3:4* shows how a leader in his church must manage his house and teach his children to be submissive. We will deal with children in the next question.

Ephesians 5:22 is the call for wives to submit to their husbands. There is a legitimate recognition that someone is over you. There is a militaristic hierarchy here; someone actually outranks you. Submission from the wife to her husband takes place in the home hierarchy and in a Christian community. As the Lord refers to the wife submitting to her husband as a piece of her Christianity, the wife's motive is to submit to Jesus and, therefore, submit to the leadership of her husband. Creation was put in place for the wife to be submissive to the husband. God ordained this in the Garden of Eden.

Ephesians 5:23 shows us that the model for submission from a wife to her husband is realized in the life of Jesus and the church. As the church is to submit to Christ as the leader, the wife is to submit to her husband as the leader. *Ephesians 5:24* says that a wife is to submit to her husband in all things. *All things* do not include abusive, immoral, or illegal behavior. In these circumstances, wives are to obey the commands of God. *Acts 5:29* instructs us to obey God rather than man.

Ephesians 5:25–29 is the commandment and pattern for husbands to love their wives. If we genuinely love our wives, we are not tyrants. *Agape* is the Greek word here for love. This signifies a mindful, cognitive decision to love. Love here is given without demands or expectations. Husbands are to model this for their wives. As much as Christ loves the church, a husband is to love his wife.

Ephesians 5:31 is the final thought on this topic. It should be noted that Paul quotes from *Genesis 2:24*. There is a clear understanding that husband and wife are to become one flesh. The husband is told to leave all other relationships, as secondary, and concentrate on his marriage. The marriage union is not superficial in gain. Marriage is sacred in the eyes of God, and effort must be put into it by the husband. As the husband leads with the love of God, in the marriage, the wife will follow the example.

Biblical responsibilities of the parents and children

At the outset of viewing *Ephesians 6*, it is clear that children, who are still under the roof of their parents' home, are to obey their parents. The natural inclination is for all people to disobey. For parents, there is a responsibility to raise children in a godly home. In order for children to learn obedience, obedience must be taught. *Proverbs 22:6* commands parents to train children in a godly context. When this is fulfilled, children will follow these teachings. Obedience is required so as to keep the child from getting into harm's way and moving into an adult life of quiet desperation.

As we teach and model obedience in the home, children will attempt to obey God. When disobedience occurs, this must be corrected. This is paralleled by the God-to-child-of-God relationship. *Proverbs 3:11* says that we should never detest God's correction in our lives. Children should never detest correction from their earthly father. However, ungodly leadership by parents to children must not be tolerated. Children are placed into an exceedingly difficult situation when their parents are sinful in the parenting process. As the term says in *Ephesians 6:1*, in the Lord, we know that biblical obedience is required of children. But in order for biblical obedience to exist, biblical parenting must also exist.

Colossians 3:21 and *Ephesians 6:4* directly tell fathers to not provoke their children. When fathers provoke their children, disobedience may be the end result. As parents, we are never to cause our children to become resentful. In the Greek text for this verse, there is a sense of bitterness creeping into the life of a child to be disobedient when they are provoked by their fathers. When godly leadership exists in the home, then *Colossians 3:20* is possible. *Ephesians 6:4* states that godly training and correction must be present in the home. These verses challenge children to obey their parents as God is then pleased with this outcome. Godly relations must be present in the home.

Adult children do not owe obedience to their parents. There is a time in everyone's life when they need to take direct responsibility for their submission to God. There is, however, an ongoing honor that is required of all children toward their parents. This honor is, in reality, a duty first and foremost to a Holy God.

Divorce may be necessary

Malachi 2:16 says that God hates divorce. This is a comprehensive, biblically based principle. God's choice for a marriage is that husbands and wives reconcile in all areas of life and stay together for life. Having stated this, it is understood that divorce does take place both in the secular arena and in the Christian community. When divorce occurs, in the Christian community, is it permitted in the presence of a Holy God?

Matthew 5:31–32 claims that divorce is permissible when sexual immorality exists in the marriage. In the Greek text, the word *porneia* is present. Translation from Greek to English of *porneia* shows that any piece of sexual immorality in a marriage, including adultery, may cause divorce in this context. As an example, it could be said that a husband, who causes his wife to move into sexual immorality, could be subjugated to her claim for a divorce.

Luke 16:18 would suggest that even though divorce may have occurred, in the eyes of God, the marriage still exists. It is therefore applied, as mentioned above, that divorce is permissible within the context of sexual immorality. God has allowed individuals to flee all sinful desires. *Galatians 5:16* instructs us to not walk in the lust of the flesh. If correction cannot occur within a Christian marriage, in terms of sexual immorality, then God allows divorce.

Under the law in *Deuteronomy 24:1–4*, divorce was easily permissible. *Mark 10:2–9* speaks of Jesus's rejection of this standard. He challenges the Pharisees on their claim for divorce. In *verse 9 of Mark 10*, Jesus says that what God has joined together, men are not allowed to separate. *Matthew 19:3–8* is a parallel scripture to ratify this claim. In *Matthew 19:9*, Jesus says that divorce is only permitted for sexual immorality. Jesus knew that God the Father had put in place the institution of marriage, and man was not to interfere with this union.

The scripture *Corinthians 7:10–11* tells us that divorce should not take place. If divorce does occur, then remarriage is not to take place. If a spouse dies, in other words, separation has not occurred due to divorce, remarriage is permitted according to *1 Corinthians 7:39*. In this circumstance, adultery has not occurred.

The scripture *1 Corinthians 7:15* does say that an unbelieving spouse has the right to choose to stay in the marriage union or leave on their own. For some, this portion of scripture shows abandonment in the marriage. When this takes place, it appears that the remaining Christian spouse is free to divorce the nonbelieving, abandoning spouse. This is why church discipline and the spiritual leaders of a local church need to be involved to assist in achieving an accurate determination.

In the case of abuse in the marriage, it could be stated that the offending spouse is not keeping with the commandment of being one flesh, with the non-offending spouse. It could be said that fleeing an abusive relationship is permitted in the eyes of God. In *Matthew 2:13–15*, we see the example of Joseph being instructed by an angel of God to flee the onslaught of Herod.

There is the approach of fleeing abusive situations. This challenge to Joseph was to avoid the Christ-child from being executed. *Psalm 55:19* calls those who do not change their lives and lack godliness as being our enemies. In an abusive marriage, the perpetrator is an enemy of the marriage union. We must be very careful about what is framed as abuse in our culture. Spiritual leaders of the church need to have active involvement.

First Corinthians 5:9–13 is a challenge for us to not keep company with those who oppose God. An abusive spouse opposes God. It could be said that we are not to keep company with those who will not submit to God and treat their spouse as one flesh.

Biblical counseling must be Christ-centered

John 14:8–9 is a striking scripture. "Philip says to Jesus, 'Show us the Father and we will be satisfied'... Jesus rebukes Philip and says, 'If you have seen me you have seen the Father.'" There is pure assurance in this text that Jesus is all we need. As Philip had requested, for the satisfaction of his soul, we have received contentment for the adequacy of Jesus only, through His ministry. The word of God is evidence that Jesus is all we need.

As a member of a Christian counseling organization, which embraces secular psychotherapy, this writer is taken aback when he considers how little regard there is, within this group, to introduce Jesus to counselees. An example is given with regard to the indifference of talking about Jesus in this context. Some time ago, a ranking official of the Christian counseling group, to which this writer belongs, sent an email of inquiry regarding the use of Jesus's wisdom in counseling. "Has anyone ever talked about Jesus in a counseling setting? If you have talked about Jesus, how did you introduce Him into the conversation?" Immediately, this writer knew that his organization of choice did not adequately embrace the truth that Jesus is enough. How might a leader, in a Christian counseling organization, struggle with bringing the life of Jesus into Christian counseling? *Colossians 1:28* instructs us to present Jesus to all men.

Man-centered counseling leans on secular psychotherapy to cure the ills of society. *Colossians 2:8* gives a stark warning; philosophy and empty deceit, the traditions of man, will deceive and distract. These teachings are of this world and not according to Jesus Christ. *Second Peter 2:20* claims that the knowledge of Jesus Christ will allow people to escape the pollution and sin of this world.

As we study the word of God, we quickly realize that it is only through the shed blood of Jesus and the working of the Holy Spirit that a person might truly find healing. When we sit with a counselee, we are assisting the Holy Spirit in His ministry. We must always strive toward discipleship. When discipleship is the focus, spiritual healing is the outcome. *John 14:26* tells us that the Holy Spirit will teach us *all* things. If this is true, all things do not include man-centered psychotherapy. *John 10:10* further states that Jesus has come to give life more abundantly. When we see the truth in this verse, we will affirm that Jesus is more than enough. Man has nothing further to offer.

Psychotherapy avoids truth and has the predisposition to mask a counselee's problems. Truth and the realization of brokenness through sin cause the counselee to seek spiritual healing. When psychotherapy explores a counselee's past life, looking for answers to the future, blame is the institute that is discovered. Did my parents love me enough? Was my family of origin a healthy environment? Am I being mindful and present at the moment? Does God really concern Himself with my sin, or does He merely love me for who I am?

As biblically based counselors, we are not therapists. There is not anything we do that can bring healing to sinful man. Man-centered therapy, therefore, has nothing to offer. *Second Corinthians 1* reminds us that when we directly suffer, our comfort and consolation come only through Jesus Christ. When we are pressed on all sides, even to the point of death (*2 Corinthians 4:7–12*), God the Father delivers us. We set our hope on Him. For this hope to be implemented into the life of a counselee, the Holy Spirit must be at work. For this hope to occur, Christ, not man, must be the center of counseling. When Biblical counseling is Christ-centered, His words bring comfort and healing.

All scripture is profitable for doctrine, reproof, and correction (*2 Timothy 3:16–17*). Comfort and healing come into the life of the counselee when he is confronted with his sin. Jesus comforted the adulterous woman in *John 8*. His future hope for her was stated in the words, "Go and sin no more."

CHRISTIANITY AND THE LAW OF SEPARATION

There is no offer of future hope when the wisdom of man is involved in the counseling process. It is clear that Jesus and nothing else is the solution for the ills of mankind. *John 1:12* outlines the fact that Christ-centered belief allows all to become children of God. He gives us the power to become His children.

APPENDIX

Purpose and Intention of Accurate and Contextual Hermeneutics

Satan wants the Christian community to misrepresent the word of God. Satan wants the Christian community to misunderstand and inappropriately apply the word of God through hermeneutical fallacies, hermeneutical errors, and exegetical blunders.

By altering God's intentions for His word, Satan has the Christian community off their task of worshipping God and doing His will. It is due to these statements that, as a Christian community, we must place extreme importance on the direction of an accurate hermeneutical-exegetical methodology for the word of God. When hermeneutics goes awry, all matters of doctrine creep into the body of Christ.

Main idea (Example)

Hermeneutical text: Proverbs 18:21
NLT: The tongue can bring death or life; those who love to talk will reap the consequences.

NKJV: Death and life are in the power of the tongue, And those who love it will eat its fruit.

HCSB: Life and death are in the power of the tongue, and those who love it will eat its fruit.

Darby's English Translation: Death and life are in the power of the tongue, and they that love it shall eat the fruit thereof.

Author: Solomon (and/or others)

Dated to the tenth century BC

Genre: Wisdom literature—poetry

For those who read this passage of scripture, the cautionary theme contained within is to be careful with our words. Words will bring life to the hearer, or words will bring death to the hearer. Proverbs 18:21 is not a verse that causes us to declare positive outcomes in our life. No, the underlying principle for the Christian community in Proverbs 18:21 is to have good fruit stored within the regenerated person so that their (our) speech will be edifying to the body of Christ. Be careful with what you say.

Here is a sample analysis of an approach to biblical hermeneutics.

Introduction

At the outset of this study, it would be beneficial to briefly provide a straightforward understanding of Proverbs 18:21. The writer of this paper will initially state the underlying principle and personal translation.

This verse is cautioning people who hold a loose tongue to be extremely careful with their words. The tongue and its speech may bring life in a metaphorical sense to one's soul, or it may bring death, also in a metaphorical sense, to the soul. Those who speak with love and concern, in godliness, will be satisfied with positive results. Wisdom literature, including Proverbs 18:21, develops character within the regenerated Christian heart.

Encoding and decoding positive understandings of the word of God are healthy for our souls. Why then is it important to concern ourselves with the need to understand the Bible at its root level? Why do we care about the interpretation of one verse, namely Proverbs 18:21? Are we not merely allowed to take any verse of the Bible and apply the verse to the Christian experience? Christians should care deeply about this thought since accuracy, when interpreting God's words, along with the adjoining presentation of the interpretation is vital to the Christian community. The body of work below will further exegete Proverbs 18:21.

Context of Scripture Reference (Strategies)

Commencing in the tenth century BC, the book of Proverbs was written as a collection of wisdom articles. Although credited to King Solomon, Proverbs may indeed have had several contributing authors. Britannica online claims: "Proverbs is probably the oldest extant document of the Hebrew wisdom movement, of which King Solomon was the founder and patron. Wisdom literature flourished throughout the ancient Near East, with Egyptian examples dating back to before the middle of the 3rd millennium BCE."[22]

---

[22] Retrieved May 29, 2021, https://www.britannica.com/topic/biblical-literature/Proverbs#ref597825.

Whereas the book of Proverbs commences with the statement, "The Proverbs of Solomon, Son of David King of Israel," Proverbs 22:17 and 24:23 would suggest additional wise sages were contributors to the content of Proverbs. While commentators may claim that Solomon wrote most of the Proverbs,[23] in truth, the precise author of Proverbs 18 may never be known to the modern reader. Nevertheless, *The New Bible Dictionary* does assert that Solomon likely was the author of Proverbs 10–22. [24]

Regardless of the exact authorship of Proverbs 18, we do know from the word of God that Solomon was indeed wise. First Kings 10:24 claims, "Now all the earth sought the presence of Solomon to hear his wisdom, which God had put on his heart." It is, therefore, not a revelation that Solomon was engaged with the book of Proverbs. As for the audience, American Theologian Bruce Waltke claims Proverbs was written to gullible tenth-century youth and wise children.[25]

The historical-cultural context tells us that the book of Proverbs was written during the tenth century BC. During this time, Palestine was ruled by the house of David. The scriptures 1 Kings and both 1 and 2 Chronicles tell us that Solomon, being the son of David, was ruling under the House of David. "These texts depict him (Solomon) as a builder, administrator, patron of wisdom, and diplomat. According to the literary traditions about Solomon, these instruments

---

[23] Retrieved June 1, 2021, https://www.Biblestudy.org/basicart/book of proverbs-overview.html.
[24] J. D. Douglas, PhD, organizing Editor, *The New Bible Dictionary* (Grand Rapids, MI: Eerdmans, 1962), 1049.
[25] Bruce Waltke, PhD, *The Book of Proverbs: Chapters 1–15. New International Commentary on the Old Testament* (Grand Rapids, MI: Eerdmans, 2005).

of rule, common to ancient Near Eastern monarchs, allowed him to consolidate the power he inherited, although he was unable to pass it to his son."[26]

Literary Context, Content, and Application

It would appear that the youth of the tenth century BC were predictable youth with regard to their behaviors. Youth of the tenth century BC and youth of the twenty-first century AD may often respond to examinations without placing much thought into their rebuttals. Therefore, the literary content, as we consider Waltke's abovementioned assertion, was for the youth of the tenth century to think before they speak. Followers of Yahweh would have wisdom available to them, which was not offered to pagans of the tenth century BC. Therefore, if youth were the intended audience, they were being encouraged to have godly fruit within their soul. The fruit of their personalities may provide life to individuals with whom they would communicate.

Conclusion

During this brief presentation, this writer employed formal equivalence to complete a word-by-word translation of Proverbs 18:21. As support for this translation, *Green's Interlinear Bible* was applied to the text.[27] Green has further utilized *Strong's Concordance* numbers above each word.

---

[26] Retrieved June 1, 2021, https://www.oxfordbibliographies.com/view/document/obo-9780195393361/obo-9780195393361-0127.xml.

[27] Jay Green Sr., PhD, *The Interlinear Bible: Hebrew-Greek-English* (Peabody, MA: Hendrickson, 2012).

Specific to this verse, we see the literary device of developmental parallelism being used. Line 2 of the Proverbs 18:21 builds on the statement of line 1.

We also recognize as we study Proverbs that the cultural and contextual river is narrow and shallow. Therefore, Proverbs 18:21 is easy to apply to the twenty-first-century church. "The book of Proverbs is perhaps the easiest of the wisdom books to understand because it speaks to such common, everyday aspects of life: work, friendship, marriage, speech, money and integrity."[28] Furthermore, for thought, this writer would suggest that understanding Proverbs 18:21 and contextualizing this verse in the twenty-first-century church are easier than attempting to apply the same strategies to the book of Revelation, which is categorized as apocalyptic literature.

Proverbs is a tapestry of wise counsel and extraordinary thought from God the creator. While there are several genres of education, in terms of literary devices utilized within the Bible, it is felt by this writer that wisdom literature steadily serves to guide the cognitive processes of the twenty-first-century church. Naturally, this is not to say that other genres do not formulate the same grounds of belief. However, wise counsel is an ongoing necessity required to guide twenty-first-century Christians.

---

[28] J. Scott Duvall, PhD, and J. Daniel Hays, PhD, *Grasping God's Word—A Hands-on Approach to Reading, Interpreting, and Applying the Bible*, Fourth Edition (Grand Rapids, MI: Zondervan, 2001).

ANNOTATED BIBLIOGRAPHY

Commentaries

Waltke, Bruce, PhD. *The Book of Proverbs: Chapters 1–15. New International Commentary on the Old Testament.* Grand Rapids, MI: Eerdmans, 2004.

Interlinear Bible

Green, Jay Sr., PhD, ed. *The Interlinear Bible: Hebrew-Greek-English.* Peabody, MA: Hendrickson, 2012.

Dictionaries

Douglas, J. D., PhD, organizing ed. *The New Bible Dictionary.* Grand Rapids, MI: Eerdmans, 1962.

Textbooks

Duvall, J. Scott, PhD, and J. Daniel Hays, PhD. *Grasping God's Word—A Hands-on Approach to Reading, Interpreting, and Applying the Bible.* Fourth Edition. Grand Rapids, MI: Zondervan, 2001.

Websites

Bible Study, the Editors. Farmington Hills, MI. 1996. Accessed June 1, 2021. https://www.biblestudy.org.

Britannica, the Editors of Encyclopaedia. "The Proverbs." Encyclopedia Britannica. May 15, 2020. Accessed May 29, 2021. http://britannica.com.

Oxford Bibliographies. Mark. W. Hamilton, PhD, author. "Solomon." 2013. Accessed June 1, 2021. https://www.oxfordbibliographies.com.

ABOUT THE AUTHOR

Dr. Byron Hardy is a retired police officer having served for nearly twenty-four years with the Royal Canadian Mounted Police and Saskatoon Police Service. He has also served as senior pastor in three churches.

At the present time, he lives in the Swan Valley of beautiful Manitoba, with his wife, Darlene, of thirty-eight years. They have two beautiful adult children, a daughter and a son, who have married great spouses. Byron and Darlene also have four adorable grandsons.

Byron and Darlene continue to be bivocational, working in ministry, while also being employed at a local wood mill.